Learning YARN

Moving beyond MapReduce—learn resource management and big data processing using YARN

Akhil Arora

Shrey Mehrotra

PUBLISHING

BIRMINGHAM - MUMBAI

Learning YARN

Copyright © 2015 Packt Publishing

First published: August 2015

Production reference: 1210815

Published by Packt Publishing Ltd.
Livery Place
35 Livery Street
Birmingham B3 2PB, UK.

ISBN 978-1-78439-396-0

www.packtpub.com

Credits

About the Authors

Akhil Arora works as a senior software engineer with Impetus Infotech and has around 5 years of extensive research and development experience. He joined Impetus Infotech in October 2012 and is working with the innovation labs team. He is a technology expert, good learner, and creative thinker. He is also passionate and enthusiastic about application development in Hadoop and other big data technologies. He loves to explore new technologies and is always ready to work on new challenges. Akhil attained a BE degree in computer science from the Apeejay College of Engineering in Sohna, Haryana, India.

> *A beginning for a new voyage, A first step towards my passion and to gain recognition, My first book Learning YARN..!!*
>
> *-- Akhil Arora*

> I dedicate this book to my parents, who are always an inspiration for me; my wife, who is my strength; and my family and friends for their faith. Last but not least, thanks to my MacBook Pro for adding the fun element and making the entire process trouble-free.

Shrey Mehrotra has more than 5 years of IT experience, and in the past 4 years, he has gained experience in designing and architecting solutions for cloud and big data domains.

Working with big data R&D Labs, he has gained insights into Hadoop, focusing on HDFS, MapReduce, and YARN. His technical strengths also include Hive, PIG, ElasticSearch, Kafka, Sqoop, Flume, and Java. During his free time, he listens to music, watches movies, and enjoys going out with friends.

> I would like to thank my mom and dad for giving me support to accomplish anything I wanted. Also, I would like to thank my friends, who bear with me while I am busy writing.

Acknowledgments

The three Is — idea, intelligence, and invention correlate to an idea given by Shrey, implemented by Akhil, and which has been used in this book.

We are glad that we approached Packt Publishing for this book and they agreed. We would like to take this opportunity to thank Packt Publishing for providing us the platform and support to write this book.

Words can't express our gratitude to the editors for their professional advice and assistance in polishing the content. A special thanks to Susmita for her support and patience during the entire process. We would also like to thank the reviewers and the technical editor, who not only helped us improve the content, but also enabled us to think better.

About the Reviewers

P. Tomas Delvechio is an IT programmer with nearly 10 years of experience. He completed his graduation at Luján University, Argentina. For his thesis, he started to research big data trends and gained a lot of deep knowledge of the MapReduce approach and the Hadoop environment. He participated in many projects as a web developer and software designing, with PHP and Python as the main languages. In his university, he worked as an assistant for the subject computer networks and taught courses on Hadoop and MapReduce for distributed systems subjects and academic conferences. Also, he is a regular member of the staff of programmers in the same institution. In his free time, he is an enthusiastic user of free software and assists in the organization of conferences of diffusion on it.

Swapnil Salunkhe is a passionate software developer who works on big data. He has a keen interest in learning and implementing new technologies. He also has a passion for functional programming, machine learning, and working with complex datasets. He can be contacted via his Twitter handle at @swapnils10.

I'd like to thank Packt Publishing and their staff for providing me with an opportunity to contribute to this book.

Parambir Singh is a JVM/frontend programmer who has worked on a variety of applications in his 10 years of experience. He's currently employed as a senior developer with Atlassian and is working on building their cloud infrastructure.

> I would like to thank my wife, Gurleen, for her support while I was busy reviewing different chapters for this book.

Jenny (Xiao) Zhang is a technology professional in business analytics, KPIs, and big data. She helps businesses better manage, measure, report, and analyze big data to answer critical business questions and give better experiences to customers. She has written a number of blog posts at jennyxiaozhang.com on big data, Hadoop, and YARN. She constantly shares insights on big data on Twitter at @smallnaruto. She previously reviewed another YARN book called *YARN Essentials*.

> I would like to thank my dad, Michael (Tiegang) Zhang, for providing technical insights in the process of reviewing this book. Special thanks to Packt Publishing for this great opportunity.

www.PacktPub.com

Support files, eBooks, discount offers, and more

For support files and downloads related to your book, please visit www.PacktPub.com.

Did you know that Packt offers eBook versions of every book published, with PDF and ePub files available? You can upgrade to the eBook version at www.PacktPub.com and as a print book customer, you are entitled to a discount on the eBook copy. Get in touch with us at service@packtpub.com for more details.

At www.PacktPub.com, you can also read a collection of free technical articles, sign up for a range of free newsletters and receive exclusive discounts and offers on Packt books and eBooks.

https://www2.packtpub.com/books/subscription/packtlib

Do you need instant solutions to your IT questions? PacktLib is Packt's online digital book library. Here, you can search, access, and read Packt's entire library of books.

Why subscribe?

- Fully searchable across every book published by Packt
- Copy and paste, print, and bookmark content
- On demand and accessible via a web browser

Free access for Packt account holders

If you have an account with Packt at www.PacktPub.com, you can use this to access PacktLib today and view 9 entirely free books. Simply use your login credentials for immediate access.

Table of Contents

Preface

Today enterprises generate huge volumes of data. In order to provide effective services and to make smarter and intelligent decisions from these huge volumes of data, enterprises use big data analytics. In recent years, Hadoop is used for massive data storage and efficient distributed processing of data. YARN framework solves design problems faced by Hadoop 1.x framework by providing a more scalable, efficient, flexible, and highly available resource management framework for distributed data processing. It provides efficient scheduling algorithms and utility components for optimized use of resources of cluster with thousands of nodes, running millions of jobs in parallel.

In this book, you'll explore what YARN provides as a business solution for distributed resource management. You will learn to configure and manage single as well as multi-node Hadoop-YARN clusters. You will also learn about the YARN daemons – ResourceManager, NodeManager, ApplicationMaster, Container, and TimeLine server, and so on.

In subsequent chapters, you will walk through YARN application life cycle management, scheduling and application execution over a Hadoop-YARN cluster. It also covers a detailed explanation of features such as High Availability, Resource Localization, and Log Aggregation. You will learn to write and manage YARN applications with ease.

Toward the end, you will learn about the security architecture and integration of YARN with big data technologies such as Spark and Storm. This book promises conceptual as well as practical knowledge of resource management using YARN.

What this book covers

Chapter 1, Starting with YARN Basics, gives a theoretical overview of YARN, its background, and need. This chapter starts with the limitations in Hadoop 1.x that leads to the evolution of a resource management framework YARN. It also covers features provided by YARN, its architecture, and advantages of using YARN as a cluster ResourceManager for a variety of batch and real-time frameworks.

Chapter 2, Setting up a Hadoop-YARN Cluster, provides a step-by-step process to set up Hadoop-YARN single-node and multi-node clusters, configuration of different YARN components and an overview of YARN's web user interface.

Chapter 3, Administering a Hadoop-YARN Cluster, provides a detailed explanation of the administrative and user commands provided by YARN. It also provides how to guides for configuring YARN, enable log aggregation, auxiliary services, Ganglia integration, JMX monitoring, and health management, and so on.

Chapter 4, Executing Applications Using YARN, explains the process of executing a YARN application over Hadoop-YARN cluster and monitoring it. This chapter describes the application flow and how the components interact during an application execution in a cluster.

Chapter 5, Understanding YARN Life Cycle Management, gives a detailed description of internal classes involved and their core functionalities. It will help readers to understand internals of state transitions of services involved in the YARN application. It will also help in troubleshooting the failures and examining the current application state.

Chapter 6, Migrating from MRv1 to MRv2, involves the steps and configuration changes required to migrate from MRv1 to MRv2 (YARN). Showcase the enhancements made in MRv2 scheduling, job management, and how to re-use MRv1 jobs in YARN. An introduction to MRv2 components integrated with YARN such as MR Job History Server and Application Master.

Chapter 7, Writing Your Own YARN Applications, describes the steps to write your own YARN applications. This includes Java code snippets for various application components definition and order of execution. It also includes detailed explanation of YARN API for creating YARN applications.

Chapter 8, Dive Deep into YARN Components, provides a detailed description of various YARN components, their roles and responsibilities. It'll also covers an overview of additional features provided by YARN such as resource localization, log management, auxiliary services, and so on.

Chapter 9, Exploring YARN REST Services, provides a detailed description of REST-based web services provided by YARN and how we can use the REST services in our applications.

Chapter 10, Scheduling YARN Applications, gives a detailed explanation of Scheduler and Queues provided by YARN for better and efficient scheduling of YARN applications. This chapter also covers the limitations of scheduling in Hadoop 1.x and how the new scheduling framework optimizing the cluster resource utilization.

Chapter 11, Enabling Security in YARN, explains the component and application-level security provided by YARN. It also gives an overview of YARN security architecture for interprocess, intercomponent communication, and token management.

Chapter 12, Real-time Data Analytics Using YARN, explains YARN adoption as a resource manager by various real-time analytics tools such as Apache Spark, Storm, and Giraph.

What you need for this book

In this book, the following are the software applications required:

- Operating systems:
    - Any Linux operating system (Ubuntu or CentOS)
    - If you wish to choose Windows, then you need to use Oracle VirtualBox to create Linux VM on the Windows machine

- Software Frameworks:
    - Java (1.6 or higher)
    - Apache Hadoop (2.5.1 or higher)
    - Apache Spark (1.1.1 or higher)
    - Apache Storm (0.9.2 or higher)

- Development Environment:
    - Eclipse IDE for Java

Who this book is for

Yet Another Resource Negotiator (YARN) is a resource management framework currently integrated with major big data technologies such as Hadoop, Spark, Storm, and so on. People working on big data can use YARN for real-time, as well as batch-oriented data analysis. This book is intended for those who want to understand what YARN is and how efficiently it is used for resource management of large clusters. For cluster administrators, it gives a detailed explanation to provision and manager YARN clusters. If you are a Java developer or an open source contributor, this book will help you drill down the YARN architecture, application execution phases, and application development in YARN. It also helps big data engineers to explore YARN integration with real-time analytics technologies such as Spark, Storm, and so on. This book is a complete package for YARN, starting with YARN's basics and taking things forward to enable readers to create their own YARN applications and integrate with other technologies.

Conventions

In this book, you will find a number of text styles that distinguish between different kinds of information. Here are some examples of these styles and an explanation of their meaning.

Code words in text, database table names, folder names, filenames, file extensions, pathnames, dummy URLs, user input, and Twitter handles are shown as follows: " This chapter uses the Apache `tar.gz` bundles for setting up Hadoop-YARN clusters and gives an overview of Hortonworks and Cloudera installations."

A block of code is set as follows:

```
<property>
    <name>fs.defaultFS</name>
    <value>hdfs://localhost:8020</value>
    <final>true</final>
</property>
```

Any command-line input or output is written as follows:

```
hdfs namenode -format
```

New terms and **important words** are shown in bold. Words that you see on the screen, for example, in menus or dialog boxes, appear in the text like this: "View the list of **DataNodes** connected to the NameNode"

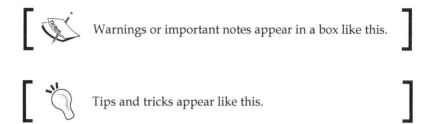

Warnings or important notes appear in a box like this.

Tips and tricks appear like this.

Reader feedback

Feedback from our readers is always welcome. Let us know what you think about this book—what you liked or disliked. Reader feedback is important for us as it helps us develop titles that you will really get the most out of.

To send us general feedback, simply e-mail feedback@packtpub.com, and mention the book's title in the subject of your message.

If there is a topic that you have expertise in and you are interested in either writing or contributing to a book, see our author guide at www.packtpub.com/authors.

Customer support

Now that you are the proud owner of a Packt book, we have a number of things to help you to get the most from your purchase.

Downloading the example code

You can download the example code files from your account at http://www.packtpub.com for all the Packt Publishing books you have purchased. If you purchased this book elsewhere, you can visit http://www.packtpub.com/support and register to have the files e-mailed directly to you.

Errata

Although we have taken every care to ensure the accuracy of our content, mistakes do happen. If you find a mistake in one of our books—maybe a mistake in the text or the code—we would be grateful if you could report this to us. By doing so, you can save other readers from frustration and help us improve subsequent versions of this book. If you find any errata, please report them by visiting http://www.packtpub.com/submit-errata, selecting your book, clicking on the **Errata Submission Form** link, and entering the details of your errata. Once your errata are verified, your submission will be accepted and the errata will be uploaded to our website or added to any list of existing errata under the Errata section of that title.

To view the previously submitted errata, go to https://www.packtpub.com/books/content/support and enter the name of the book in the search field. The required information will appear under the **Errata** section.

Piracy

Piracy of copyrighted material on the Internet is an ongoing problem across all media. At Packt, we take the protection of our copyright and licenses very seriously. If you come across any illegal copies of our works in any form on the Internet, please provide us with the location address or website name immediately so that we can pursue a remedy.

Please contact us at copyright@packtpub.com with a link to the suspected pirated material.

We appreciate your help in protecting our authors and our ability to bring you valuable content.

Questions

If you have a problem with any aspect of this book, you can contact us at questions@packtpub.com, and we will do our best to address the problem.

1
Starting with YARN Basics

In early 2006, Apache Hadoop was introduced as a framework for the distributed processing of large datasets stored across clusters of computers, using a programming model. Hadoop was developed as a solution to handle big data in a cost effective and easiest way possible. Hadoop consisted of a storage layer, that is, **Hadoop Distributed File System** (**HDFS**) and the MapReduce framework for managing resource utilization and job execution on a cluster. With the ability to deliver high performance parallel data analysis and to work with commodity hardware, Hadoop is used for big data analysis and batch processing of historical data through MapReduce programming.

With the exponential increase in the usage of social networking sites such as Facebook, Twitter, and LinkedIn and e-commerce sites such as Amazon, there was the need of a framework to support not only MapReduce batch processing, but real-time and interactive data analysis as well. Enterprises should be able to execute other applications over the cluster to ensure that cluster capabilities are utilized to the fullest. The data storage framework of Hadoop was able to counter the growing data size, but resource management became a bottleneck. The resource management framework for Hadoop needed a new design to solve the growing needs of big data.

YARN, an acronym for **Yet Another Resource Negotiator**, has been introduced as a second-generation resource management framework for Hadoop. YARN is added as a subproject of Apache Hadoop. With MapReduce focusing only on batch processing, YARN is designed to provide a generic processing platform for data stored across a cluster and a robust cluster resource management framework.

In this chapter, we will cover the following topics:

- Introduction to MapReduce v1
- Shortcomings of MapReduce v1
- An overview of the YARN components

- The YARN architecture
- How YARN satisfies big data needs
- Projects powered by YARN

Introduction to MapReduce v1

MapReduce is a software framework used to write applications that simultaneously process vast amounts of data on large clusters of commodity hardware in a reliable, fault-tolerant manner. It is a batch-oriented model where a large amount of data is stored in Hadoop Distributed File System (HDFS), and the computation on data is performed as MapReduce phases. The basic principle for the MapReduce framework is to move computed data rather than move data over the network for computation. The MapReduce tasks are scheduled to run on the same physical nodes on which data resides. This significantly reduces the network traffic and keeps most of the I/O on the local disk or within the same rack.

The high-level architecture of the MapReduce framework has three main modules:

- **MapReduce API**: This is the end-user API used for programming the MapReduce jobs to be executed on the HDFS data.
- **MapReduce framework**: This is the runtime implementation of various phases in a MapReduce job such as the map, sort/shuffle/merge aggregation, and reduce phases.
- **MapReduce system**: This is the backend infrastructure required to run the user's MapReduce application, manage cluster resources, schedule thousands of concurrent jobs, and so on.

The MapReduce system consists of two components—JobTracker and TaskTracker.

- JobTracker is the master daemon within Hadoop that is responsible for resource management, job scheduling, and management. The responsibilities are as follows:
    - Hadoop clients communicate with the JobTracker to submit or kill jobs and poll for jobs' progress
    - JobTracker validates the client request and if validated, then it allocates the TaskTracker nodes for map-reduce tasks execution
    - JobTracker monitors TaskTracker nodes and their resource utilization, that is, how many tasks are currently running, the count of map-reduce task slots available, decides whether the TaskTracker node needs to be marked as blacklisted node, and so on

- JobTracker monitors the progress of jobs and if a job/task fails, it automatically reinitializes the job/task on a different TaskTracker node

- JobTracker also keeps the history of the jobs executed on the cluster

- **TaskTracker** is a per node daemon responsible for the execution of map-reduce tasks. A TaskTracker node is configured to accept a number of map-reduce tasks from the JobTracker, that is, the total map-reduce tasks a TaskTracker can execute simultaneously. The responsibilities are as follows:

  - TaskTracker initializes a new JVM process to perform the MapReduce logic. Running a task on a separate JVM ensures that the task failure does not harm the health of the TaskTracker daemon.

  - TaskTracker monitors these JVM processes and updates the task progress to the JobTracker on regular intervals.

  - TaskTracker also sends a heartbeat signal and its current resource utilization metric (available task slots) to the JobTracker every few minutes.

Shortcomings of MapReducev1

Though the Hadoop MapReduce framework was widely used, the following are the limitations that were found with the framework:

- **Batch processing only**: The resources across the cluster are tightly coupled with map-reduce programming. It does not support integration of other data processing frameworks and forces everything to look like a MapReduce job. The emerging customer requirements demand support for real-time and near real-time processing on the data stored on the distributed file systems.

- **Nonscalability and inefficiency**: The MapReduce framework completely depends on the master daemon, that is, the JobTracker. It manages the cluster resources, execution of jobs, and fault tolerance as well.

  It is observed that the Hadoop cluster performance degrades drastically when the cluster size increases above 4,000 nodes or the count of concurrent tasks crosses 40,000. The centralized handling of jobs control flow resulted in endless scalability concerns for the scheduler.

- **Unavailability and unreliability**: The availability and reliability are considered to be critical aspects of a framework such as Hadoop. A single point of failure for the MapReduce framework is the failure of the JobTracker daemon. The JobTracker manages the jobs and resources across the cluster. If it goes down, information related to the running or queued jobs and the job history is lost. The queued and running jobs are killed if the JobTracker fails. The MapReduce v1 framework doesn't have any provision to recover the lost data or jobs.

- **Partitioning of resources**: A MapReduce framework divides a job into multiple map and reduce tasks. The nodes with running the TaskTracker daemon are considered as resources. The capability of a resource to execute MapReduce jobs is expressed as the number of map-reduce tasks a resource can execute simultaneously. The framework forced the cluster resources to be partitioned into map and reduce task slots. Such partitioning of the resources resulted in less utilization of the cluster resources.

hadoop1namenode Hadoop Machine List

Active Task Trackers

					Task Trackers					
Name	Host	# running tasks	Max Map Tasks	Max Reduce Tasks	Task Failures	Directory Failures	Node Health Status	Seconds Since Node Last Healthy	Total Tasks Since Start	Succeeded Tasks Since Start
tracker_hadoop1namenode:127.0.0.1/127.0.0.1:58113	hadoop1namenode	0	2	2	0	0	N/A	0	0	0

> If you have a running Hadoop 1.x cluster, you can refer to the JobTracker web interface to view the map and reduce task slots of the active TaskTracker nodes.
>
> The link for the active TaskTracker list is as follows:
> `http://JobTrackerHost:50030/machines.jsp?type=active`

- **Management of user logs and job resources**: The user logs refer to the logs generated by a MapReduce job. Logs for MapReduce jobs. These logs can be used to validate the correctness of a job or to perform log analysis to tune up the job's performance. In MapReduce v1, the user logs are generated and stored on the local file system of the slave nodes. Accessing logs on the slaves is a pain as users might not have the permissions issued. Since logs were stored on the local file system of a slave, in case the disk goes down, the logs will be lost.

A MapReduce job might require some extra resources for job execution. In the MapReduce v1 framework, the client copies job resources to the HDFS with the replication of 10. Accessing resources remotely or through HDFS is not efficient. Thus, there's a need for localization of resources and a robust framework to manage job resources.

In January 2008, Arun C. Murthy logged a bug in JIRA against the MapReduce architecture, which resulted in a generic resource scheduler and a per job user-defined component that manages the application execution.

You can see this at `https://issues.apache.org/jira/browse/MAPREDUCE-279`

An overview of YARN components

YARN divides the responsibilities of JobTracker into separate components, each having a specified task to perform. In Hadoop-1, the JobTracker takes care of resource management, job scheduling, and job monitoring. YARN divides these responsibilities of JobTracker into ResourceManager and ApplicationMaster. Instead of TaskTracker, it uses NodeManager as the worker daemon for execution of map-reduce tasks. The ResourceManager and the NodeManager form the computation framework for YARN, and ApplicationMaster is an application-specific framework for application management.

ResourceManager
- A per-cluster service
- Authority that arbitrates resources among all the applications in the system.
- Has a pluggable scheduler for cluster resource optimization & an ApplicationsManager

NodeManager
- A per-machine framework agent / the "worker" daemon in YARN
- Creates applications' execution container, monitors their resource usage and reports to the ResourceManager

ApplicationMaster
- A per-application framework specific library
- Negotiates resources from the ResourceManager
- Works with the NodeManager(s) to execute and monitor the tasks

ResourceManager

A ResourceManager is a per cluster service that manages the scheduling of compute resources to applications. It optimizes cluster utilization in terms of memory, CPU cores, fairness, and SLAs. To allow different policy constraints, it has algorithms in terms of pluggable schedulers such as capacity and fair that allows resource allocation in a particular way.

ResourceManager has two main components:

- **Scheduler**: This is a pure pluggable component that is only responsible for allocating resources to applications submitted to the cluster, applying constraint of capacities and queues. Scheduler does not provide any guarantee for job completion or monitoring, it only allocates the cluster resources governed by the nature of job and resource requirement.

- **ApplicationsManager (AsM)**: This is a service used to manage application masters across the cluster that is responsible for accepting the application submission, providing the resources for application master to start, monitoring the application progress, and restart, in case of application failure.

NodeManager

The NodeManager is a per node worker service that is responsible for the execution of containers based on the node capacity. Node capacity is calculated based on the installed memory and the number of CPU cores. The NodeManager service sends a heartbeat signal to the ResourceManager to update its health status. The NodeManager service is similar to the TaskTracker service in MapReduce v1. NodeManager also sends the status to ResourceManager, which could be the status of the node on which it is running or the status of tasks executing on it.

ApplicationMaster

An ApplicationMaster is a per application framework-specific library that manages each instance of an application that runs within YARN. YARN treats ApplicationMaster as a third-party library responsible for negotiating the resources from the ResourceManager scheduler and works with NodeManager to execute the tasks. The ResourceManager allocates containers to the ApplicationMaster and these containers are then used to run the application-specific processes. ApplicationMaster also tracks the status of the application and monitors the progress of the containers. When the execution of a container gets complete, the ApplicationMaster unregisters the containers with the ResourceManager and unregisters itself after the execution of the application is complete.

Container

A container is a logical bundle of resources in terms of memory, CPU, disk, and so on that is bound to a particular node. In the first version of YARN, a container is equivalent to a block of memory. The ResourceManager scheduler service dynamically allocates resources as containers. A container grants rights to an ApplicationMaster to use a specific amount of resources of a specific host. An ApplicationMaster is considered as the first container of an application and it manages the execution of the application logic on allocated containers.

The YARN architecture

In the previous topic, we discussed the YARN components. Here we'll discuss the high-level architecture of YARN and look at how the components interact with each other.

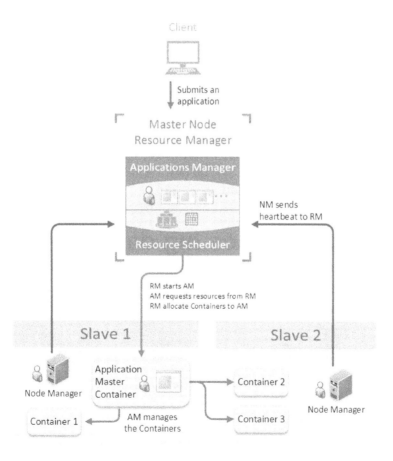

The ResourceManager service runs on the master node of the cluster. A YARN client submits an application to the ResourceManager. An application can be a single MapReduce job, a directed acyclic graph of jobs, a java application, or any shell script. The client also defines an ApplicationMaster and a command to start the ApplicationMaster on a node.

The ApplicationManager service of resource manager will validate and accept the application request from the client. The scheduler service of resource manager will allocate a container for the ApplicationMaster on a node and the NodeManager service on that node will use the command to start the ApplicationMaster service. Each YARN application has a special container called ApplicationMaster. The ApplicationMaster container is the first container of an application.

The ApplicationMaster requests resources from the ResourceManager. The RequestRequest will have the location of the node, memory, and CPU cores required. The ResourceManager will allocate the resources as containers on a set of nodes. The ApplicationMaster will connect to the NodeManager services and request NodeManager to start containers. The ApplicationMaster manages the execution of the containers and will notify the ResourceManager once the application execution is over. Application execution and progress monitoring is the responsibility of ApplicationMaster rather than ResourceManager.

The NodeManager service runs on each slave of the YARN cluster. It is responsible for running application's containers. The resources specified for a container are taken from the NodeManager resources. Each NodeManager periodically updates ResourceManager for the set of available resources. The ResourceManager scheduler service uses this resource matrix to allocate new containers to ApplicationMaster or to start execution of a new application.

How YARN satisfies big data needs

We talked about the MapReduce v1 framework and some limitations of the framework. Let's now discuss how YARN solves these issues:

Non-Scalability and
Inefficiency

Unavailability and
Unreliability

Scalability and High Cluster Utilization

High Availability for Components

Partitioning of
Resources

YARN

Flexible Resource Model

Multiple Data Processing Algorithms

Batch-Processing Only

Log Aggression and Resource Localization

Management of User
Logs and Job Resources

- **Scalability and higher cluster utilization**: Scalability is the ability of a software or product to implement well under an expanding workload. In YARN, the responsibility of resource management and job scheduling / monitoring is divided into separate daemons, allowing YARN daemons to scale the cluster without degrading the performance of the cluster.

  With a flexible and generic resource model in YARN, the scheduler handles an overall resource profile for each type of application. This structure makes the communication and storage of resource requests efficient for the scheduler resulting in higher cluster utilization.

- **High availability for components**: Fault tolerance is a core design principle for any multitenancy platform such as YARN. This responsibility is delegated to ResourceManager and ApplicationMaster. The application specific framework, ApplicationMaster, handles the failure of a container. The ResourceManager handles the failure of NodeManager and ApplicationMaster.

- **Flexible resource model**: In MapReduce v1, resources are defined as the number of map and reduce task slots available for the execution of a job. Every resource request cannot be mapped as map/reduce slots. In YARN, a resource-request is defined in terms of memory, CPU, locality, and so on. It results in a generic definition for a resource request by an application. The NodeManager node is the worker node and its capability is calculated based on the installed memory and cores of the CPU.

- **Multiple data processing algorithms**: The MapReduce framework is bounded to batch processing only. YARN is developed with a need to perform a wide variety of data processing over the data stored over Hadoop HDFS. YARN is a framework for generic resource management and allows users to execute multiple data processing algorithms over the data.

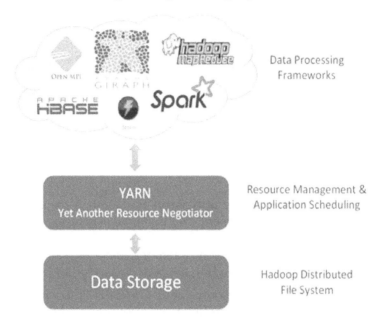

- **Log aggregation and resource localization**: As discussed earlier, accessing and managing user logs is difficult in the Hadoop 1.x framework. To manage user logs, YARN introduced a concept of log aggregation. In YARN, once the application is finished, the NodeManager service aggregates the user logs related to an application and these aggregated logs are written out to a single log file in HDFS. To access the logs, users can use either the YARN command-line options, YARN web interface, or can fetch directly from HDFS.

A container might require external resources such as jars, files, or scripts on a local file system. These are made available to containers before they are started. An ApplicationMaster defines a list of resources that are required to run the containers. For efficient disk utilization and access security, the NodeManager ensures the availability of specified resources and their deletion after use.

Projects powered by YARN

Efficient and reliable resource management is a basic need of a distributed application framework. YARN provides a generic resource management framework to support data analysis through multiple data processing algorithms. There are a lot of projects that have started using YARN for resource management. We've listed a few of these projects here and discussed how YARN integration solves their business requirements:

- **Apache Giraph**: Giraph is a framework for offline batch processing of semistructured graph data stored using Hadoop. With the Hadoop 1.x version, Giraph had no control over the scheduling policies, heap memory of the mappers, and locality awareness for the running job. Also, defining a Giraph job on the basis of mappers / reducers slots was a bottleneck. YARN's flexible resource allocation model, locality awareness principle, and application master framework ease the Giraph's job management and resource allocation to tasks.

- **Apache Spark**: Spark enables iterative data processing and machine learning algorithms to perform analysis over data available through HDFS, HBase, or other storage systems. Spark uses YARN's resource management capabilities and framework to submit the DAG of a job. The spark user can focus more on data analytics' use cases rather than how spark is integrated with Hadoop or how jobs are executed.

Some other projects powered by YARN are as follows:

- **MapReduce**: https://issues.apache.org/jira/browse/MAPREDUCE-279
- **Giraph**: https://issues.apache.org/jira/browse/GIRAPH-13
- **Spark**: http://spark.apache.org/
- **OpenMPI**: https://issues.apache.org/jira/browse/MAPREDUCE-2911
- **HAMA**: https://issues.apache.org/jira/browse/HAMA-431
- **HBase**: https://issues.apache.org/jira/browse/HBASE-4329
- **Storm**: http://hortonworks.com/labs/storm/

 A page on Hadoop wiki lists a number of projects/applications that are migrating to or using YARN as their resource management tool. You can see this at http://wiki.apache.org/hadoop/PoweredByYarn.

Summary

It is time to summarize the learning from this chapter and let you know what's to come in the next chapter. In this chapter, you learnt about the MapReduce v1 framework and its shortcomings. The chapter also covered an introduction to YARN, its components, architecture, and different projects powered by YARN. It also explained how YARN solves big data needs. In the next chapter, you will create single as well as multiple node Hadoop-YARN clusters and begin with your first step to YARN.

2
Setting up a Hadoop-YARN Cluster

YARN is a subproject of Apache Hadoop at the Apache Software Foundation, introduced in the Hadoop 2.0 version. YARN replaces the old MapReduce framework of the Hadoop 1.x version and is shipped with the Hadoop 2.x bundle. This chapter will provide a step-by-step guide for Hadoop-YARN users to install and configure YARN with Hadoop.

A Hadoop-YARN cluster can be configured as a single node as well as a multi-node cluster. This chapter covers both types of installations along with the troubleshooting guidelines. This chapter helps YARN beginners and the cluster administrators easily configure Hadoop-YARN clusters and understand how YARN components interact with each other.

Apache, Hortonworks, and Cloudera are the main distributors of Hadoop. These vendors have their own steps to install and configure Hadoop-YARN clusters. This chapter uses the Apache `tar.gz` bundles for setting up Hadoop-YARN clusters and gives an overview of Hortonworks and Cloudera installations.

In this chapter, we will cover the following topics:

- The supported platforms, hardware and software requirements, and basic Linux commands
- How to prepare a node while setting up a cluster
- A single node installation
- Overview of Hadoop HDFS and YARN ResourceManager web-UI
- Testing your cluster
- Multi-node installation
- Overview of Hortonworks and Cloudera installations

Starting with the basics

The Apache Hadoop 2.x version consists of three key components:

- Hadoop Distributed File System (HDFS)
- Yet Another Resource Negotiator (YARN)
- The MapReduce API (Job execution, MRApplicationMaster, JobHistoryServer, and so on)

There are two master processes that manage the Hadoop 2.x cluster—the NameNode and the ResourceManager. All the slave nodes in the cluster have DataNode and NodeManager processes running as the worker daemons for the cluster. The NameNode and DataNode daemons are part of HDFS, whereas the ResourceManager and NodeManager belong to YARN.

When we configure Hadoop-YARN on a single node, we need to have all four processes running on the same system. Hadoop single node installation is generally used for learning purposes. If you are a beginner and need to understand the Hadoop-YARN concepts, you can use a single node Hadoop-YARN cluster.

In the production environment, a multi-node cluster is used. It is recommended to have separate nodes for NameNode and ResourceManager daemons. As the number of slave nodes in the cluster increases, the requirement of memory, processor, and network of the master nodes increases. The following diagram shows the high-level view of Hadoop-YARN processes running on a multi-node cluster.

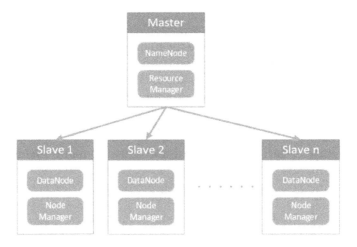

Supported platforms

To install a Hadoop-YARN cluster, you can use either GNU-, Linux-, or Windows-based operating systems. The steps to configure and use the Hadoop-YARN cluster for these operating systems are different. It is recommended to use GNU/Linux for your cluster installations. Apache Hadoop is an open source framework and it's widely used on open source platforms such as Ubuntu/CentOS. The support documents and blogs for Linux machines are easily available. Some companies use the enterprise version of Linux systems such as RHEL (RedHat Enterprise Linux).

In this chapter, we'll be using a 64-bit Ubuntu Desktop (version 14.04) for deployment of the Hadoop-YARN cluster. You can download an ISO image for Ubuntu Desktop from its official website (`http://www.ubuntu.com/download`).

Hardware requirements

The following section covers the recommended hardware configuration to run Apache Hadoop.

For learning purpose, nodes in the cluster must have the following:

* 1.5 or 2 GB of RAM
* 15-20 GB free hard disk.

If you don't have physical machines, you can use a tool such as Oracle Virtualbox to host virtual machines on your host system. To know more about Oracle Virtualbox and how to install virtual machines using Oracle Virtualbox, you can refer to the blog at `http://www.protechskills.com/big-data/hadoop/administration/create-new-vm-using-oracle-virtualbox`.

To select nodes for a production environment, you can refer to a blog on the Hortonworks website at `http://hortonworks.com/blog/best-practices-for-selecting-apache-hadoop-hardware/`.

Software requirements

Hadoop is an open source framework that requires:

* Java already installed on all the nodes
* A passwordless SSH from the master node to the slave nodes

The steps to install java and configure passwordless SSH are covered later in the chapter.

Basic Linux commands / utilities

Before moving forward, it is important to understand the usage of the following Linux commands:

- Sudo
- Nano editor
- Source
- Jps
- Netstat
- Man

The official documentation for the Hadoop cluster installation is based on the Linux platform and as mentioned in the previous section, Linux OS is preferred over the Windows OS. This section allows readers with minimum knowledge of Linux to deploy a Hadoop-YARN cluster with ease. Readers new to Linux should have basic knowledge of these commands / utilities before moving to the cluster installation steps. This section of the chapter covers an overview and usage of these commands.

Sudo

In Linux, the `sudo` command allows a user to execute a command as a superuser, or in other words an administrator of a windows system. The file `/etc/sudoers` contains a list of users who have the `sudo` permission. If you need to change any of the system properties or access any system file, you need to add `sudo` in the beginning of the command. To read more about the `sudo` command, you can refer to the blog at `http://www.tutorialspoint.com/unix_commands/sudo.htm`.

Nano editor

Nano is one of the editor tools for Linux. Its ease of use and simplicity allow beginners to handle files easily. To read more about the `nano` editor, you can refer to the documentation at `http://www.nano-editor.org/dist/v2.0/nano.html`.

The alternate to the `nano` editor is the default `vi` editor.

Source

When you edit any of the environment setting files such as `/etc/environment` or `~/.bashrc`, you need to refresh the file to apply the changes made in the file without restarting the system. To read more about the `source` command, you can refer to the blog at `http://bash.cyberciti.biz/guide/Source_command`.

Jps

Jps is a Java command used to list the Java processes running on a system. The output of the command contains the process ID and process name for all of the Java processes. Before using the jps command, you need to make sure that the bin directory of your JAVA_HOME command is set in the PATH variable for the user.

A sample output is as follows:

```
hduser@host:~$ jps
6690 Jps
2071 ResourceManager
2471 NameNode
```

To read more about the jps command, you can refer to the Oracle documentation at http://docs.oracle.com/javase/7/docs/technotes/tools/share/jps.html.

Netstat

The netstat command is a utility to list the active ports on a system. It checks for TCP and UDP connections. This command will be helpful to get the list of ports being used by a process. To read more about the netstat command and its options, you can refer to the blog at http://www.c-jump.com/CIS24/Slides/Networking/html_utils/netstat.html.

You can use the netstat command with the grep command to get filtered results for a particular process:

```
netstat -nlp | grep <PID>
```

Man

Most of the Linux commands have their documentations and user manuals that are also known as *man pages*. The man command is used to format and view these man pages through the command line interface. The basic syntax of the man command is as follows:

- **Syntax**: man [option(s)] keyword(s)
- **Example**: man ls

To read more about the man command, you can refer to the wiki page at http://en.wikipedia.org/wiki/Man_page

Preparing a node for a Hadoop-YARN cluster

Before using a machine as a Hadoop node in a cluster, there are a few prerequisites that need to be configured.

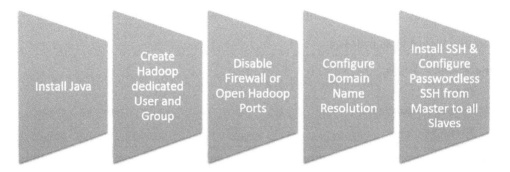

Install Java

As mentioned in the software requirements for a cluster, all the nodes across the cluster must have Sun Java 1.6 or above and the SSH service installed. The Java version and JAVA_HOME should be consistent across all the nodes. If you want to read more regarding the Java compatibility with Hadoop, you can browse to a page on wiki at `http://wiki.apache.org/hadoop/HadoopJavaVersions`.

To install and configure Java on Ubuntu, you can refer to the blog at `http://www.protechskills.com/linux/unix-commands/install-java-in-linux`.

- To verify if Java is installed, you can execute the following command:

  `java -version`

- The Java version will be displayed on the console. The output of the command will look like this:

  ```
  java version "1.8.0"
  Java(TM) SE Runtime Environment (build 1.8.0-b132)
  Java HotSpot(TM) 64-Bit Server VM (build 25.0-b70, mixed
  mode)
  ```

- To verify that the environment variable for Java is configured properly, execute the following command:

  `echo $JAVA_HOME`

- The installation directory for Java will be displayed on the console. The output of the command will look like this:

  `/usr/lib/jvm/jdk1.8.0/`

Create a Hadoop dedicated user and group

In the Hadoop cluster node installation, the Hadoop daemons run on multiple systems. The slave nodes run the DataNode and NodeManager services. All the nodes in a cluster must have a common user and a group. It is recommended to create a dedicated user for the Hadoop cluster on all the nodes of your cluster.

To create a user on Ubuntu, you can refer to the Ubuntu documentation at `http://manpages.ubuntu.com/manpages/jaunty/man8/useradd.8.html`.

Here is a sample command to create a new user `hduser` on Ubuntu:

```
sudo usersadd -m hduser
```

After creating a new user, you also need to set a password for the new user. Execute the following command to set a password for the newly created user `hduser`:

```
sudo passwd hduser
```

Disable firewall or open Hadoop ports

Hadoop daemons use a few ports for internal and client communication. The cluster administrator has an option to either disable the firewall of the nodes or allow traffic on the ports required by Hadoop. Hadoop has a list of default ports, but you can configure them as per your need.

To disable the firewall in Ubuntu, execute the following command:

```
sudo ufw disable
```

Here are some useful links for the ports to be used and firewall options available:

`http://www.cloudera.com/content/cloudera-content/cloudera-docs/CM4Ent/4.5.2/Configuring-Ports-for-Cloudera-Manager-Enterprise-Edition/cmeecp_topic_3.html`

`http://docs.hortonworks.com/HDPDocuments/HDP1/HDP-1.2.0/bk_reference/content/reference_chap2_1.html`

`http://www.protechskills.com/linux/ubuntu/ubuntu-firewall`

`http://wiki.centos.org/HowTos/Network/IPTables`

Configure the domain name resolution

A Hadoop node is identified through its hostname. All the nodes in the cluster must have a unique hostname and IP address. Each Hadoop node should be able to resolve the hostname of the other nodes in the cluster.

If you are not using a DHCP server that manages your DNS hostname resolution, then you need to configure the /etc/hosts file on all the nodes. The /etc/hosts file of a system contains the IP addresses of the nodes specified with their hostname. You need to prepend the file with the IP address and hostname mapping. You can use the *nano* or *vi* editor with the sudo option to edit the file contents. Assuming the hostname of your nodes is master, slave1, slave2, and so on; the contents of the file will look similar to the following:

```
192.168.56.100      master
192.168.56.101      slave1
192.168.56.102      slave2
192.168.56.103      slave3
```

To view the system hostname, you can execute the hostname command.

```
hostname
```

To modify the system hostname in Linux, you can refer to the blogs here:

CentOS: https://www.centosblog.com/how-to-change-hostname-on-centos-linux/

Ubuntu: http://askubuntu.com/questions/87665/how-do-i-change-the-hostname-without-a-restart

After editing the file, you need to either restart your system network settings or reboot your system.

To restart networking on Ubuntu, execute the following command:

```
sudo /etc/init.d/networking restart
```

To verify that configuration is working properly, execute the following command:

```
ping slave1
```

To stop the command, press *ctrl* + *c*. The output of the command will look like this:

```
PING slave1 (slave1) 56(84) bytes of data.
64 bytes from slave1: icmp_req=1 ttl=64 time=0.025 ms
64 bytes from slave1: icmp_req=2 ttl=64 time=0.024 ms
```

Install SSH and configure passwordless SSH from the master to all slaves

The OpenSSH server and client packages should already be installed and the `sshd` service should be running on all the nodes. By default, the `sshd` service uses port 22.

To install these packages on Ubuntu, execute the following commands:

```
sudo apt-get install openssh-client
sudo apt-get install openssh-server
```

The Hadoop master node remotely manages all the Hadoop daemons running across the cluster. The master node creates a secure connection through SSH using the dedicated user group for the cluster. It is recommended that you allow the master node to create an SSH connection without a password. You need to configure a passwordless SSH from the master node to all slave nodes.

First you need to create SSH keys for the master node, then share the master's public key with the target slave node using the `ssh-copy-id` command.

Assuming that the user for the Hadoop-YARN cluster is `hduser`, the `ssh-copy-id` command will append the contents of the master node's public key file, `/home/hduser/.ssh/ id_dsa.pub`, to the `/home/hduser/.ssh/authorized_keys` file on the slave node.

To install the SSH service and configure a passwordless SSH on Ubuntu, you can refer to the Ubuntu documentation at `https://help.ubuntu.com/lts/serverguide/openssh-server.html`.

To verify that the `sshd` service is running, execute the following `netstat` command:

```
sudo netstat -nlp | grep sshd
```

The output will contain the service details if the service is running:

```
tcp   0   0 0.0.0.0:22   0.0.0.0:*   LISTEN   670/sshd
```

To verify the passwordless SSH connection, execute the `ssh` command from the master node and observe that the command will not prompt for a password now:

```
ssh hduser@slave1
```

The Hadoop-YARN single node installation

In a single node installation, all the Hadoop-YARN daemons (NameNode, ResourceManager, DataNode, and NodeManager) run on a single node as separate Java processes. You will need only one Linux machine with a minimum of 2 GB RAM and 15 GB free disk space.

Prerequisites

Before starting with the installation steps, make sure that you prepare the node as specified in the above topic.

- The hostname used in the single node installation is `localhost` with `127.0.0.1` as the IP address. It is known as the loopback address for a machine. You need to make sure that the `/etc/hosts` file contains the resolution for the loopback address. The loopback entry will look like this:

  ```
  127.0.0.1     localhost
  ```

- The passwordless SSH is configured for `localhost`. To ensure this, execute the following command:

  ```
  ssh-copy-id localhost
  ```

Installation steps

After preparing your node for Hadoop, you need to follow a simple five-step process to install and run Hadoop on your Linux machine.

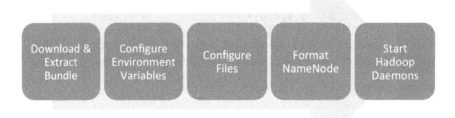

Step 1 – Download and extract the Hadoop bundle

The current version of Hadoop is 2.5.1 and the steps mentioned here will assume that you use the same version. Login to your system using a Hadoop dedicated user and download the Hadoop 2.x bundle `tar.gz` file from the Apache archive:

```
wget https://archive.apache.org/dist/hadoop/core/hadoop-2.5.1/hadoop-
2.5.1.tar.gz
```

You can use your `home` directory for the Hadoop installation (`/home/<username>`). If you want to use any of the system directories such as `/opt` or `/usr` for installation, you need to use the `sudo` option with the commands. For simplicity, we'll install Hadoop in the home directory of the user. The commands in this chapter assume that the username is `hduser`. You can replace `hduser` with the actual username. Move your Hadoop bundle to the user's `home` directory and extract the contents of the bundle file:

```
mv hadoop-2.5.1.tar.gz /home/hduser/
cd /home/hduser
tar -xzvf hadoop-2.5.1.tar.gz
```

Step 2 – Configure the environment variables

Configure the Hadoop environment variables in `/home/hduser/.bashrc` (for Ubuntu) or `/home/hduser/.bash_profile` (for CentOS). Hadoop requires the `HADOOP_PREFIX` and `home` directory environment variables to be set before starting Hadoop services. `HADOOP_PREFIX` specifies the installation directory for Hadoop. We assume that you extracted the Hadoop bundle in the `home` folder of `hduser`.

Use the nano editor and append the following export commands to the end of the file:

```
export HADOOP_PREFIX="/home/hduser/hadoop-2.5.1/"
export PATH=$PATH:$HADOOP_PREFIX/bin
export PATH=$PATH:$HADOOP_PREFIX/sbin
export HADOOP_COMMON_HOME=${HADOOP_PREFIX}
export HADOOP_MAPRED_HOME=${HADOOP_PREFIX}
export HADOOP_HDFS_HOME=${HADOOP_PREFIX}
export YARN_HOME=${HADOOP_PREFIX}
```

After saving the file, you need to refresh the file using the `source` command:

```
source ~/.bashrc
```

Step 3 – Configure the Hadoop configuration files

Next, you need to configure the Hadoop site configuration files. There are four configuration files that you need to update. You can find these files in the `$HADOOP_PREFIX/etc/Hadoop` folder.

The core-site.xml file

The `core-site.xml` file contains information for the `namenode` host and the RPC port used by NameNode. For a single node installation, the host for `namenode` will be `localhost`. The default RPC port for NameNode is `8020`. You need to edit the file and add a configuration property under the configuration tag:

```
<property>
    <name>fs.defaultFS</name>
    <value>hdfs://localhost:8020</value>
    <final>true</final>
</property>
```

The hdfs-site.xml file

The `hdfs-site.xml` file contains the configuration properties related to HDFS. In this file, you specify the replication factor and the directories for `namenode` and `datanode` to store their data. Edit the `hdfs-site.xml` file and add the following properties under the configuration tag:

```
<property>
    <name>dfs.replication</name>
    <value>1</value>
</property>

<property>
    <name>dfs.namenode.name.dir</name>
    <value>file:///home/hduser/hadoop-
2.5.1/hadoop_data/dfs/name</value>
</property>

<property>
    <name>dfs.datanode.data.dir</name>
    <value>file:///home/hduser/hadoop-
2.5.1/hadoop_data/dfs/data</value>
</property>
```

The mapred-site.xml file

The `mapred-site.xml` file contains information related to the MapReduce framework for the cluster. You will specify the framework to be configured as `yarn`. The other possible values for the MapReduce framework property are `local` and `classic`. A detailed explanation of these values is given in the next chapter.

In the Hadoop configuration folder, you will find a template for the `mapred-site.xml` file. Execute the following command to copy the template file to create the `mapred-site.xml` file:

cp /home/hduser/hadoop2.5.1/etc/Hadoop/mapred-site.xml.template /home/hduser/hadoop2.5.1/etc/Hadoop/mapred-site.xml

Now edit the `mapred-site.xml` file and add the following properties under the configuration tag:

```
<property>
   <name>mapreduce.framework.name</name>
   <value>yarn</value>
</property>
```

The yarn-site.xml file

The `yarn-site.xml` file contains the information related to the YARN daemons and YARN properties. You need to specify the host and port for the `resourcemanager` daemon. Similar to the NameNode host, for a single node installation, the value for a ResourceManager host is `localhost`. The default RPC port for ResourceManager is `8032`. You also need to specify the scheduler to be used by ResourceManager and auxiliary services for `nodemanager`. We'll cover these properties in detail in the next chapter. Edit the `yarn-site.xml` file and add the following properties under the configuration tag:

```
<property>
    <name>yarn.resourcemanager.address</name>
    <value>localhost:8032</value>
</property>

<property>
    <name>yarn.resourcemanager.scheduler.address</name>
    <value>localhost:8030</value>
</property>

<property>
    <name>yarn.resourcemanager.resource-tracker.address</name>
    <value>localhost:8031</value>
</property>
```

```
<property>
    <name>yarn.resourcemanager.admin.address</name>
    <value>localhost:8033</value>
</property>

<property>
    <name>yarn.resourcemanager.webapp.address</name>
    <value>localhost:8088</value>
</property>

<property>
    <name>yarn.nodemanager.aux-services</name>
    <value>mapreduce_shuffle</value>
</property>

<property>
    <name>yarn.nodemanager.aux-
services.mapreduce_shuffle.class</name>
    <value>org.apache.hadoop.mapred.ShuffleHandler</value>
</property>

<property>
    <name>yarn.resourcemanager.scheduler.class</name>
    <value>org.apache.hadoop.yarn.server.resourcemanager.scheduler.cap
acity.CapacityScheduler</value>
</property>
```

The hadoop-env.sh and yarn-env.sh files

The Hadoop daemons require Java settings to be set in the Hadoop environment files. You need to configure the value for JAVA_HOME (the java installation directory) in the Hadoop and YARN environment files. Open the hadoop-env.sh and yarn-env.sh files, uncomment the export JAVA_HOME command, and update the export command with the actual JAVA_HOME value. To uncomment the export command, just remove the # symbol from the line.

The slaves file

The slaves file contains a list of hostname for slave nodes. For single node installation, the value of host is localhost. By default, the slaves file contains only localhost. You don't need to modify the slaves file for a single node installation.

Step 4 – Format NameNode

After configuring Hadoop files, you need to format the HDFS using the `namenode` format command. Before executing the format command, make sure that the `dfs.namenode.name.dir` directory specified in the `hdfs-site.xml` file does not exist. This directory is created by the `namenode` format command. Execute the following command to format NameNode:

```
hdfs namenode -format
```

After executing the preceding command, make sure that there's no exception on the console and that the `namenode` directory is created.

> The following line in the console output specifies that the `namenode` directory has been successfully formatted:
>
> `INFO common.Storage:` Storage directory `/home/hduser/hadoop-2.5.1/hadoop_data/dfs/name` has been successfully formatted.

Step 5 – Start Hadoop daemons

Start the Hadoop services using Hadoop 2 Scripts in the `/home/hduser/hadoop-2.5.1/sbin/` directory. For a single node installation, all the daemons will run on a single system. Use the following commands to start the services one by one.

Service	Command
NameNode	`hadoop-daemon.sh start namenode`
DataNode	`hadoop-daemon.sh start datanode`
ResourceManager	`yarn-daemon.sh start resourcemanager`
NodeManager	`yarn-daemon.sh start nodemanager`

Execute the `jps` command and ensure that all Hadoop daemons are running. You can also verify the status of your cluster through the web interface for HDFS-NameNode and YARN-ResourceManager.

Service	URL
HDFS-NameNode	`http://<NameNodeHost>:50070/`
YARN-ResourceManager	`http://<ResourceManagerHost>:8088/`

You need to replace `<NameNodeHost>` and `<ResourceManagerHost>` with `localhost` for single node installation such as `http://localhost:8088/`.

An overview of web user interfaces

Similar to web interfaces available in the Hadoop 1.x version, the Hadoop 2.x version has web user interfaces for Hadoop services. Instead of the `JobTracker` service web UI, the web UI for ResourceManager is used to monitor applications and resources. A detailed explanation regarding the configurations related to the web UI's is given in the next chapter.

The following screenshot refers to the web-interface of Hadoop HDFS. Through the HDFS interface, you can:

- Explore the HDFS metrics
- View the list of **DataNodes** connected to the NameNode
- Browse the file system, and so on

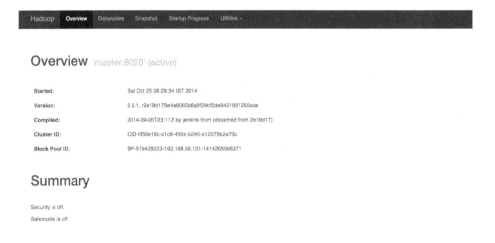

The following screenshot refers to the web-interface of YARN ResourceManager. It shows:

- A summarized view of the cluster resource capabilities
- A list of applications related to the cluster
- A list of NodeManager nodes connected
- The scheduler details, and so on

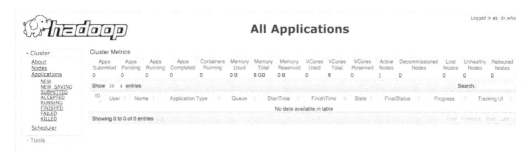

You can refer to the .pid files for the Hadoop daemons that are created in the /tmp folder of your node. These files contain the current process ID for each daemon:

```
Testhdfs dfs -mkdir -p /user/hduser/input
```

```
hdfs dfs -copyFromLocal /home/hduser/hadoop-2.5.1/etc/hadoop/*
/user/hduser/input
```

To verify that your files are successfully copied into HDFS, execute the following command or browse to the HDFS filesystem through the HDFS web UI at http://localhost:50070/explorer.html:

```
hdfs dfs -ls /user/hduser/input
```

Run a sample application

Hadoop uses the yarn command to submit an application to the cluster. You can find the yarn command in the /home/hduser/hadoop-2.5.1/bin folder and the examples jar file containing sample MapReduce applications in the /home/hduser/hadoop-2.5.1/share/hadoop/mapreduce folder. Other than the examples jar path, specify three arguments to the command—the operation to perform (word count), the HDFS input directory, and an HDFS directory to store the output of the MapReduce application. Ensure that the HDFS output directory does not exist.

Execute the following command to run a word count example:

```
yarn jar /home/hduser/hadoop-2.5.1/share/hadoop/mapreduce/hadoop-
mapreduce-examples-2.5.1.jar wordcount /user/hduser/input
/user/hduser/output
```

Monitor the progress of the application through the YARN web user-interface at `http://localhost:8088/cluster/apps`

The Hadoop-YARN multi-node installation

Installing a multi-node Hadoop-YARN cluster is similar to a single node installation. You need to configure the master node, the same as you did during the single node installation. Then, copy the Hadoop installation directory to all the slave nodes and set the Hadoop environment variables for the slave nodes. You can start the Hadoop daemons either directly from the master node, or you can login to each node to run their respective services.

Prerequisites

Before starting with the installation steps, make sure that you prepare all the nodes as specified here:

- All the nodes in the cluster have a unique hostname and IP address. Each node should be able to identify all other nodes through the hostname. If you are not using the DHCP server, you need to make sure that the `/etc/hosts` file contains the resolution for all nodes used in the cluster. The entries will look similar to the following:

  ```
  192.168.56.101    master
  192.168.56.102    slave1
  192.168.56.103    slave2
  192.168.56.104    slave3
  ```

- Passwordless SSH is configured from the master to all the slave nodes in the cluster. To ensure this, execute the following command on the master for all the slave nodes:

  ```
  ssh-copy-id <SlaveHostName>
  ```

Installation steps

After preparing your nodes as per the Hadoop multi-node cluster installation, you need to follow a simple six-step process to install and run Hadoop on your Linux machine. To better understand the process, you can refer to the following diagram:

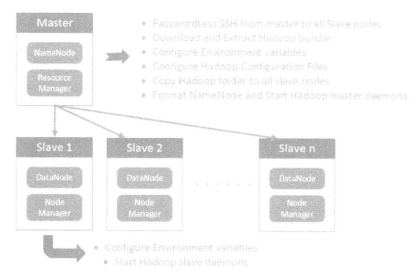

Step 1 – Configure the master node as a single-node Hadoop-YARN installation

You need to follow the first three steps mentioned in the installation steps for the Hadoop-YARN single node installation. The main difference while configuring the node for the multi-node cluster is the usage of the master node's hostname instead of a loopback hostname (`localhost`). Assuming that the hostname of the master node is `master`, you need to replace `localhost` with `master` in the `core-site.xml` and `yarn-site.xml` configuration files. The properties in these files will look as follows:

- `core-site.xml`:

```
<property>
    <name>fs.defaultFS</name>
    <value>hdfs://master:8020</value>
    <final>true</final>
</property>
```

- `yarn-site.xml`:

```
<property>
    <name>yarn.resourcemanager.address</name>
```

```
        <value>master:8032</value>
    </property>

    <property>
        <name>yarn.resourcemanager.scheduler.address</name>
        <value>master:8030</value>
    </property>

    <property>
        <name>yarn.resourcemanager.resource-tracker.address</name>
        <value>master:8031</value>
    </property>

    <property>
        <name>yarn.resourcemanager.admin.address</name>
        <value>master:8033</value>
    </property>

    <property>
        <name>yarn.resourcemanager.webapp.address</name>
        <value>master:8088</value>
    </property>

    <property>
        <name>yarn.nodemanager.aux-services</name>
        <value>mapreduce_shuffle</value>
    </property>

    <property>
        <name>yarn.nodemanager.aux-services.mapreduce_shuffle.class</
name>
        <value>org.apache.hadoop.mapred.ShuffleHandler</value>
    </property>

    <property>
        <name>yarn.resourcemanager.scheduler.class</name>
        <value>org.apache.hadoop.yarn.server.resourcemanager.
scheduler.capacity.CapacityScheduler</value>
    </property>
```

You also need to modify the slaves file. As mentioned earlier, it contains the list of all the slave nodes. You need to add a hostname for all the slave nodes to the slaves file. The content of the file will look as follows:

```
slave1
slave2
slave3
```

Step 2 – Copy the Hadoop folder to all the slave nodes

After configuring your master node, you need to copy the `HADOOP_PREFIX` directory to all the slave nodes. The location of the Hadoop directory and the Hadoop configuration files should be in sync with the master node. You can use the `scp` command to securely copy files from master to all slaves:

```
for node in 'cat <path_for_slaves_file in hadoop_conf_directory>'; do
  scp -r <hadoop_dir> $node:<parent_directory of hadoop_dir>; done
```

After replacing the path used in the preceding command with valid directories, the command will look as follows:

```
for node in 'cat /home/hduser/hadoop-
2.5.1/etc/hadoop/slaves'; do scp
  -r /home/hduser/hadoop-2.5.1 $node:/home/hduser;
done
```

If you are using any system directory as a Hadoop directory (a directory that requires a `sudo` option for any write operation, for example, `/opt`), then you will have to use the `rsync` utility to copy the Hadoop folder to all the slave nodes. It requires **NOPASSWD: ALL** enabled for the user on the slave machines. You can refer to the blog at `http://www.ducea.com/2006/06/18/linux-tips-password-usage-in-sudo-passwd-nopasswd/`. This ensures that the user is not prompted for any password while running sudo:

```
for node in `cat <path_for_slaves_file in hadoop_conf_directory>`; do
  sudo rsync --rsync-path="sudo rsync" -r <hadoop_dir>
$node:<parent_directory of hadoop_dir>; done
```

Step 3 – Configure environment variables on slave nodes

Similar to configuring the Hadoop environment variables on the master node, you need to configure the environment variables in all the slave nodes. You need to login to the slave node, edit the `/home/hduser/.bashrc` file and recompile the file using the `source` command. You can also refer to step 2, under the installation steps for the Hadoop-YARN single node installation.

Step 4 – Format NameNode

This step is the same as you followed for the single node installation. You need to login to the master node and execute the `hdfs format` command. For more details, you can refer to step 4, under the installation steps for the Hadoop-YARN single node installation.

Step 5 – Start Hadoop daemons

The configuration for the Hadoop-YARN multi node cluster is now finished. Now you need to start the Hadoop-YARN daemons. Login to the master node and run the master daemons (NameNode and ResourceManager) using the below scripts:

Service	Command
NameNode	`hadoop-daemon.sh start namenode`
ResourceManager	`yarn-daemon.sh start resourcemanager`

Login to each slave node and execute the following scripts to start the DataNode and NodeManager daemons.

Service	Command
DataNode	`hadoop-daemon.sh start datanode`
NodeManager	`yarn-daemon.sh start nodemanager`

If you are configuring a large cluster, then executing the scripts on all the slave nodes is time consuming. To help cluster administrators, Hadoop provides scripts to `start` / `stop` all Hadoop daemons through the master node. You need to login to the master node and execute the following scripts to `start` / `stop` the HDFS and YARN daemons respectively.

Service	Command
HDFS	`start-dfs.sh / stop-dfs.sh`
NodeManager	`start-yarn.sh / stop-yarn.sh`

You can find scripts such as `start-all.sh` and `stop-all.sh`, but the usage of these scripts is deprecated in the latest versions of Hadoop.

Execute the `jps` command on each node and ensure that all the Hadoop daemons are running. You can also verify the status of your cluster through the web interface for **HDFS-NameNode** and **YARN-ResourceManager**.

Service	Url
HDFS-NameNode	`http://master:50070/`
YARN-ResourceManager	`http://master:8088/`

To test your cluster, you can refer to the previous topic as the steps to test the multi-node cluster are exactly the same as the single node cluster.

An overview of the Hortonworks and Cloudera installations

Hortonworks and Cloudera are two main distributors of Hadoop. These distributors have their own style of installation. The installation is done as a package installation through `yum` (CentOS) or `apt-get` (Ubuntu). The directory structure is different for configuration files, log files, `.pid` files, and so on.

Both these distributors have developed tools to provision, manage, and monitor the Hadoop clusters through a web UI. Cloudera Manager from Cloudera and Apache Ambari are being used by a majority of the companies. Ambari is an open source project that lacks features such as rolling upgrades, managements of third-party libraries, and so on. Cloudera Manager is a mature product and is available in both Express and Enterprise versions.

To read more about Cloudera Manager and Ambari, you can refer to the official website at `http://www.cloudera.com/content/cloudera/en/products-and-services/cloudera-enterprise/cloudera-manager.html`.

`http://ambari.apache.org/`

Summary

In this chapter, we covered the Hadoop-YARN single as well as multi node cluster setup. We will assume that you are now familiar with the Hadoop-YARN processes and can test your cluster by running a sample MapReduce job. You can now load sample data HDFS and try to run different MapReduce jobs. You can check the progress of the running applications through the YARN web-UI and explore other options as well. In the next chapter, we'll cover the administrative part of YARN.

3

Administering a
Hadoop-YARN Cluster

In the previous chapter, we covered the installation steps to configure single and multi-node Hadoop-YARN clusters. As an administrator or a user of a Hadoop-YARN cluster, it is important to know how services are configured or managed. For example, an administrator must monitor the health of all the nodes across the cluster and a user should be able to view the logs of the applications submitted.

Hadoop-YARN has a predefined set of user, as well as administrative commands. It exposes monitoring data as service metrics and provides an easy integration of monitoring data with tools such as Ganglia, Nagios, and so on. It also defines a mechanism for High Availability and recovery.

In this chapter, we will cover:

- The YARN user and administration commands
- Configuring, managing, and monitoring YARN services
- ResourceManager's High Availability
- Monitoring NodeManager's health

Using the Hadoop-YARN commands

YARN commands are invoked using the `bin/yarn` script in the Hadoop bundle. The basic syntax for the `yarn` command is:

```
yarn [--config confdir] COMMAND COMMAND_OPTIONS
```

Running the YARN script without any arguments, prints the description for all the commands. The `config` option is optional and its default value is `$HADOOP_PREFIX/etc/hadoop`.

YARN commands are classified as user and administration commands, as shown in the following figure:

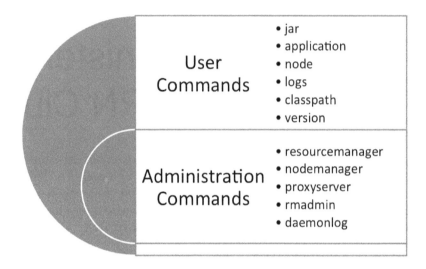

The user commands

Hadoop-YARN clients execute the user commands. These clients connect to the YARN services using the configuration settings specified in the `yarn-site.xml` file. As specified in the previous chapter, the `yarn-site.xml` file and the other configuration files are all placed in the Hadoop configuration folder (`/home/hduser/hadoop-2.5.1/etc/conf/`). There are mainly six user commands in the Hadoop-YARN framework.

Jar

The `jar` command is used to run a `jar` file with the YARN code, that is, to submit a YARN application to the ResourceManager.

- **Usage**: `yarn jar <jar_path> <mainClass> args`
- **Class**: `org.apache.hadoop.util.RunJar`

The main method of the `RunJar` class is invoked. It checks the argument list and then validates the `jar` file. It extracts the `jar` file and runs the `main` method of the Java main class specified as the second argument of this command.

Application

The `application` command is used to print the list of applications submitted to the ResourceManager by any client. It can also be used to report or kill an application.

- **Usage**: `yarn application <options>`
- **Class**: `org.apache.hadoop.yarn.client.cli.ApplicationCLI`

Command options

- `-status ApplicationId`: The `status` option is used to print the status of the application in the form of an application report. For an existing / valid application ID, it prints the data retrieved from an object of the `org.apache.hadoop.yarn.api.records.ApplicationReport` class. For a non existing application ID, it throws an `ApplicationNotFoundException`.

Sample output

```
Application Report:

Application-Id: application_1389458248889_0001

Application-Name: QuasiMonteCarlo

Application-Type: MAPREDUCE

User: Root

Queue: Default

Start-Time: 1389458385135

Finish-Time: 1389458424546

Progress: 100%

State: FINISHED

Final-State: SUCCEEDED

Tracking-URL: http://slave1:19888/jobhistory/job/job_1389458248889_0001

RPC Port: 34925

AM Host: slave3

Diagnostics:
```

- `-list -appTypes=[ ] -appStates=[ ]`: The `list` option prints the list of all the applications based on the application's type and state. It supports two sub-options, `appTypes` and `appStates`. If no option is specified, by default all the applications with the state RUNNING, ACCEPTED, SUBMITTED are listed. The user can specify the type and state filter as a comma-separated list of values (without adding a space).
    - `appTypes`: MAPREDUCE, YARN

○ appStates: ALL, NEW, NEW_SAVING, SUBMITTED, ACCEPTED, RUNNING, FINISHED, FAILED, KILLED

- -kill ApplicationId: The kill option is used to kill a running / submitted application. If the application is already finished, the state of the application is either FINISHED, KILLED, or FAILED, then it prints the message to the command line. Otherwise, it sends a kill request to the ResourceManager to kill the application.

Node

A YARN cluster consists of nodes running with the NodeManager daemon as a Java process. The ResourceManager saves the node information and the yarn node command prints the information of the node in the form of a node report using the object of the class org.apache.hadoop.yarn.api.records.NodeReport.

- **Usage**: yarn node <options>
- **Class**: org.apache.hadoop.yarn.client.cli.NodeCLI

Command options

- -status NodeId: The status option is used to print the status of a node in the form of a node report. The NodeId parameter is a string representation of an object of the org.apache.hadoop.yarn.api.records.NodeId class, that is, the combination of the node's host name and the communicating port for the node manager daemon, the IPC Server listener port. For an existing / valid node ID, it prints the data retrieved from an object of the NodeReport class.

Sample output

Node Report:

Node-Id: slave1:36801

Rack: /default-rack

Node-State: RUNNING

Node-Http-Address:slave1: 8042

Last-Health-Update: Sun 09/Feb/14 11:37:53:774IST

Health-Report:

Containers: 0

Memory-Used: 0MB

Memory-Capacity: 8192MB

CPU-Used: 0 vcores

CPU-Capacity: 8 vcores

- `-list`: The `list` option prints the list of all the nodes based on the node state. It supports an optional use of `-states` to filter the nodes based on the node state, and `-all` to list all the nodes:

    ° The user can specify the state filter as a comma-separated list of values. `org.apache.hadoop.yarn.api.records.NodeState` is an enumeration representing the different states of a node.

    ° The states are: NEW, RUNNING, UNHEALTHY, DECOMMISSIONED, LOST, REBOOTED

    ° The output of the `list` command is a list of nodes with basic information about the nodes, such as `Node-Id`, `Node-State`, `Node-Http-Address`, and the number of running containers.

Logs

The `logs` command retrieves the logs for the completed YARN applications, that is, an application in any of the following three states—FAILED, KILLED, or FINISHED.

To view the logs through the command line, the user needs to enable `log-aggregation` for the YARN cluster. To enable the `log-aggregation` feature, the user needs to set the `yarn.log-aggregation-enable` property to `true` in the `yarn-site.xml` file. The user can also view logs based on the container ID and node ID for an application.

- **Usage**: `yarn logs -applicationId <application ID> <options>`
- **Class**: `org.apache.hadoop.yarn.client.cli.LogsCLI`

Command options

- `-applicationId applicationID`: The `applicationId` command is mandatory and is used to get the application details from the resource manager.

- `-appOwner AppOwner`: It is optional and assumed to be the current user if not specified.

- `-nodeAddress NodeAddress -containerId containerId`: The `nodeAddress` and `containerId` commands can be specified to get container specific logs for a particular node. `nodeAddress` is a string in the form of `host:port` (the same as `NodeId`).

Classpath

The `classpath` command is used to print the current value of `CLASSPATH` for the YARN cluster. This command is very useful for developers and cluster administrators as it displays the list of the libraries included in the PATH while running the YARN services.

- **Usage**: `yarn classpath`
- **Script**: `echo $CLASSPATH`

Version

The `version` command is used to print the version of the deployed YARN cluster. Since YARN is tightly coupled with Hadoop, the command uses the `HadoopUtil` classes to fetch the version of the Hadoop bundle used.

- **Usage**: `yarn version`
- **Class**: `org.apache.hadoop.util.VersionInfo`

Administration commands

YARN administration commands are mainly used to start cluster services on a particular node. A cluster administrator also uses these commands to manage the cluster nodes, queues, information related to the access control list, and so on.

ResourceManager / NodeManager / ProxyServer

These commands are used to start the YARN services on a particular node. For the ResourceManager and NodeManager services, the script appends the logger properties to the `classpath` variable. To modify the log properties, the user needs to create the `log4j.properties` file in the service specific configuration directories (`rm-config` and `nm-config`) in the YARN configuration directory for the cluster. The YARN script also uses the environment variables defined for the JVM heap size configured for that service.

- **Usage**: `yarn resourcemanager`
- **Class**: `org.apache.hadoop.yarn.server.resourcemanager.ResourceManager`
- **Usage**: `yarn nodemanager`
- **Class**: `org.apache.hadoop.yarn.server.nodemanager.NodeManager`
- **Usage**: `yarn proxyserver`
- **Class**: `org.apache.hadoop.yarn.server.webproxy.WebAppProxyServer`

RMAdmin

The `rmadmin` command starts a resource manager client from the command line. It is used to refresh the access control policies, scheduler queues and the nodes registered with ResourceManager. The change in the policies is directly reflected in the YARN cluster after the `rmadmin` refresh command and the cluster does not require a restart for the associated services.

The `RMAdminCLI` class uses the YARN protobuf services to call the methods defined in the `AdminService` class in the `org.apache.hadoop.yarn.server.resourcemanager` package.

- **Usage**: `yarn rmadmin <options>`
- **Class**: `org.apache.hadoop.yarn.client.cli.RMAdminCLI`

Command options

- `-refreshQueues`: Reloads the queues' acls, states, and scheduler properties. It reinitializes the configured scheduler with the latest configuration files.

- `-refreshNodes`: Refreshes the host's information for ResourceManager. It reads the resource manager's nodes `include` and `exclude` files to update the included and excluded node lists for the cluster.

- `-refreshUserToGroupsMappings`: Based on the configured Hadoop security group mapping, it updates the user to groups mappings by refreshing the groups' cache.

- `-refreshSuperUserGroupsConfiguration`: Refreshes the superuser proxy groups mappings and update the proxy hosts and proxy groups defined in the `hadoop.proxyuser` settings in the `core-site.xml` configuration file.

- `-refreshAdminAcls`: Refreshes the access control list for administration of the resource manager defined by the `yarn.admin.acl` property in the YARN site / default configuration files.

- `-refreshServiceAcl`: Reloads the service level authorization policy file and resource manager will reload the authorization policy file. It checks whether the Hadoop security authorization is enabled and refreshes the access control lists for the following resource manager services:
  - IPC Server
  - ApplicationMaster
  - Client
  - The resource tracker

- `-help [cmd]`: Displays help for the given command or all the commands if none is specified.

DaemonLog

It is used to view or update the log level for the YARN resource manager or node manager daemons. It verifies the administrator access for the user and then internally connects to `http://host:port/logLevel?log=name` service. The port specified should be an HTTP port for the service.

- **Usage** : `yarn daemonlog <options> args`
- **Class** : `org.apache.hadoop.log.LogLevel`

Command options

- `-getLevel host:port name`: Prints the log level of the daemon
- `-setLevel host:port name level`: Sets the log level of the daemon

Configuring the Hadoop-YARN services

Hadoop-YARN services are configured using a `property` tag. A `property` tag contains the `name`, `value`, and `description` of a property. It also contains an optional flag to mark the property as final. The default values for these properties are defined in the `yarn-default.xml` file. An administrator can override the default values by defining properties in the `yarn-site.xml` file. To explore the properties in the `yarn-default.xml` file, you can refer to the link `http://hadoop.apache.org/docs/r2.5.1/hadoop-yarn/hadoop-yarn-common/yarn-default.xml`.

A YARN service is configured as a `host:port` value. The host can be the hostname or an IP address of a node. You can also specify the value of any another property using the `$` symbol with curly braces, such as `${sample.property}`.

The ResourceManager service

The hostname for the ResourceManager node is configured using the `yarn.resourcemanager.hostname` property. Its default value is `0.0.0.0` and an administrator should override its value in the `yarn-site.xml` file, as given in the following script:

```
<property>
    <name>yarn.resourcemanager.hostname</name>
    <value>ResourceManagerHost</value>
</property>
```

As we saw in the previous chapter, you can assume the value for `ResourceManagerHost` to be `master`. The ResourceManager service consists of various interfaces, such as applications manager, scheduler, admin, web application, and so on. Each of these interfaces is mapped to a particular port. An administrator can override the value of the configured port, but the value of the hostname should be the same as the `yarn.resourcemanager.hostname` value.

The following are the properties related to the ResourceManager's interfaces:

- Applications manager:

```
<property>
    <name>yarn.resourcemanager.address</name>
    <value>${yarn.resourcemanager.hostname}:8032</value>
</property>
```

- Web application-HTTP:

```
<property>
    <name>yarn.resourcemanager.webapp.address</name>
    <value>${yarn.resourcemanager.hostname}:8088</value>
</property>
```

- Web application-HTTPs:

```
<property>
    <name>yarn.resourcemanager.webapp.https.address</name>
    <value>${yarn.resourcemanager.hostname}:8090</value>
</property>
```

- Admin:

```
<property>
    <name>yarn.resourcemanager.admin.address</name>
    <value>${yarn.resourcemanager.hostname}:8033</value>
</property>
```

- Scheduler:

```
<property>
    <name>yarn.resourcemanager.scheduler.address</name>
    <value>${yarn.resourcemanager.hostname}:8030</value>
</property>
```

- The resource tracker:

```
<property>
    <name>yarn.resourcemanager.resource-tracker.address</name>
    <value>${yarn.resourcemanager.hostname}:8031</value>
</property>
```

The NodeManager service

An administrator can define the hostname of the NodeManager service by using the `yarn.nodemanager.hostname` property. The default value for this property is `0.0.0.0` and it is recommended to use the default value only. The IP address `0.0.0.0` points to the same node and this ensures consistent configuration across all the NodeManager nodes in the cluster, as given in the following script:

```
<property>
    <name>yarn.nodemanager.hostname</name>
    <value>0.0.0.0</value>
</property>
```

Similar to ResourceManager, the NodeManager service also exposes a few interfaces for internal communication. The following are the properties related to the NodeManager's interfaces:

- Container manager:

```
<property>
    <name>yarn.nodemanager.address</name>
    <value>${yarn.nodemanager.hostname}:0</value>
</property>
```

- Web Application - HTTP:

```
<property>
    <name>yarn.nodemanager.webapp.address</name>
    <value>${yarn.nodemanager.hostname}:8042</value>
</property>
```

- Localizer:

```
<property>
    <name>yarn.nodemanager.localizer.address</name>
    <value>${yarn.nodemanager.hostname}:8040</value>
</property>
```

The Timeline server

The Timeline server is a new feature in YARN. It provides generic information about the applications executed on the YARN cluster. It also exposes the `TimelineClient` class to publish application specific information. By default, this service is disabled.

An administrator can enable the Timeline server by specifying the following property in the `yarn-site.xml` file:

```
<property>
    <name>yarn.timeline-service.generic-application-
history.enabled</name>
    <value>true</value>
</property>
```

The Timeline server is a per-cluster service and an administrator needs to configure the host in the `yarn-site.xml` file. It uses an RPC port for internal communication and exposes a web application through HTTP, as well as HTTPS ports.

An administrator can configure the host for the Timeline server by using the following property:

```
<property>
    <name>yarn.timeline-service.hostname</name>
    <value>0.0.0.0</value>
</property>
```

An administrator can also configure RPC, as well as web application ports, using the following properties:

```
<property>
    <name>yarn.timeline-service.address</name>
    <value>${yarn.timeline-service.hostname}:10200</value>
</property>

<property>
    <name>yarn.timeline-service.webapp.address</name>
    <value>${yarn.timeline-service.hostname}:8188</value>
</property>

<property>
    <name>yarn.timeline-service.webapp.https.address</name>
    <value>${yarn.timeline-service.hostname}:8190</value>
</property>
```

Currently, the Timeline server is in the development phase. To read more about the Timeline server, you can refer to the Apache Hadoop documentation at `http://hadoop.apache.org/docs/r2.5.2/hadoop-yarn/hadoop-yarn-site/TimelineServer.html`.

The web application proxy server

The proxy server in YARN is embedded within the ResourceManager service by default. You can also configure the proxy server to run on a separate node. It is introduced to save the ResourceManager service and the users accessing the cluster from web based attacks. ApplicationMaster is treated as a process from an untrusted user. The links exposed by the ApplicationMaster could point to malicious external sites. YARN provides a basic implementation to warn the users about the risk of accessing the ApplicationMaster. You can configure the host and the port of the proxy server by using the configuration mentioned next:

```
<property>
    <name>yarn.web-proxy.address</name>
    <value>WebAppProxyHost:port<value>
</property>
```

If the preceding property is not specified in the `yarn-site.xml` file, then the proxy server will run with the ResourceManager service.

Ports summary

The following table defines a summarized list of default ports configured for the YARN services:

Service	Property		Default Port
ResourceManager	RPC Communication	`yarn.resourcemanager.address`	8032
	Web UI	`yarn.resourcemanager.webapp.address`	8088
	Scheduler	`yarn.resourcemanager.scheduler.address`	8030
	Resource tracker	`yarn.resourcemanager.resource-tracker.address`	8031
	Admin	`yarn.resourcemanager.admin.address`	8033
NodeManager	RPC Communication	`yarn.nodemanager.address`	8041
	Localizer	`yarn.nodemanager.localizer.address`	8040
	Web UI	`yarn.nodemanager.webapp.address`	8042

Service		Property	Default Port
TimeLine Server	RPC Communication	`yarn.timeline-service.address`	10200
	Web UI	`yarn.timeline-service.webapp.address`	8188
	HTTPS	`yarn.timeline-service.webapp.https.address`	8190

Managing the Hadoop-YARN services

The `sbin` Hadoop-YARN bundle contains shell scripts to manage the YARN services. It is always easy to use scripts to start or stop the services. It reads the required Hadoop configuration files, such as `yarn-site.xml` and `slaves`, in the `etc/hadoop/` directory. This section will cover the usage of different scripts used by YARN.

Similar to Hadoop-HDFS scripts, YARN uses four scripts, listed and described next:

- `start-yarn.sh`: The `start-yarn` script is used to start all the YARN daemons—ResourceManager, NodeManager on all slaves and the proxy server with a single script. It should be executed on the ResourceManager node, that is, the master node. It reads the slaves file in the configuration folder to get a list of the slaves in the YARN cluster. It creates a secure shell connection to each of the slave nodes and executes a command to start the NodeManager daemon on that node. It does not require any arguments.

- `stop-yarn.sh`: The `stop-yarn` script is similar to the `start-yarn.sh` script. It is used to stop all the YARN daemons with a single script.

- `yarn-daemon.sh`: The `yarn-daemon` script is used to start or stop a particular service on a node. It reads the `yarn-site.xml` file to get the value of the host. It requires two arguments: the action that needs to be performed and the service name.

  ° **Command syntax:** `yarn-daemon.sh [--config <conf-dir>] [--hosts hostlistfile] (start|stop) <yarn-command>`

  ° Other than the two required arguments, you can also specify the directory path for the configuration folder and a host file that contains the list of hosts, to start the specified service.

    °   The different values for the YARN command can be:

       `resourcemanager`

       `nodemanager`

       `proxyserver`

       `historyserver`

- `yarn-daemons.sh`: The `yarn-daemons` script is used to start or stop a particular service on all the slave nodes. It executes the `sbin/slaves.sh` file to list the slave nodes and connect to the node. An administrator can use this script to manage the NodeManager daemons on all the slave nodes with a single script.

Managing service logs

The `logs` files of each of the Hadoop-YARN services is created during the `service start` command.

The default directory for logs is the `$HADOOP_PREFIX/logs` folder. You can configure the directory location by specifying the `YARN_LOG_DIR` environment variable in the `etc/hadoop/yarn-env.sh` file. The pattern for name of a `log` file is `$YARN_LOG_DIR/yarn-$YARN_IDENT_STRING-$command-$HOSTNAME.log`. This is described as follows:

- `YARN_IDENT_STRING` is a string to identify the user name that executed the start script. Its default value is `$USER`.
- `$command` is one of the YARN commands used with the `yarn-daemon.sh` script.
- `$HOSTNAME` is the host for the YARN service.

A sample name for a `log` file will be `yarn-hduser-resourcemanager-master.log`.

Managing pid files

During service startup, a `pid` file for each service is created. This file contains the process ID for that service. The default directory to store these `pid` files is `/tmp`. You can configure the storage for the `pid` file by specifying the `YARN_PID_DIR` environment variable in the `etc/hadoop/yarn-env.sh` file. The pattern for the name of a `pid` file is similar to a `log` file. It is `$YARN_PID_DIR/yarn-$YARN_IDENT_STRING-$command.pid`.

When an administrator executes a stop script, the process ID for the specified service is fetched from the `pid` file and the script uses the `kill` command to stop the service.

Monitoring the YARN services

When we talk about handling big data and multi node clusters for distributed processing, we consider performance and efficiency as major factors. Monitoring of the YARN services includes collection of cluster, node, and service level metrics. Each of the YARN services exposes its monitoring information as JMX MBean object. As a cluster administrator, a person needs to monitor these metrics through detailed graphs and reporting tools, such as Jconsole, Ganglia, and so on. In this section, we'll discuss the different techniques used to monitor the YARN services.

JMX monitoring

JMX are the Java tools used for monitoring and managing applications, objects, and so on. The resources are represented as Managed Bean or simply MBean objects. An MBean represents a resource running in a Java Virtual Machine. The statistical information collected from these resources regarding performance, system resource usage, application events, and such, could be used to fine tune the application.

The Hadoop-YARN daemons, ResourceManager, and NodeManager provide Java Management Extensions (JMX) beans. These beans contain information about the cluster or the YARN services running on the cluster. A bean name is a composite attribute of the Hadoop-YARN service name and the information type.

The following is a sample JMX response in JSON format from NodeManager JMX URL:

```
←  ⊛ 192.168.145.182:8042/jmx                                    C  ⊠ ▾ Google

{  "beans" : [ {
    "name" : "Hadoop:service=NodeManager,name=ShuffleMetrics",
    "modelerType" : "ShuffleMetrics",
    "tag.Context" : "mapred",
    "tag.Hostname" : "IMPETUS-DSRV03.IMPETUS.CO.IN",
    "ShuffleOutputBytes" : 0,
    "ShuffleOutputsFailed" : 0,
    "ShuffleOutputsOK" : 0,
    "ShuffleConnections" : 0
  }, {
    "name" : "Hadoop:service=NodeManager,name=JvmMetrics",
    "modelerType" : "JvmMetrics",
    "tag.Context" : "jvm",
    "tag.ProcessName" : "NodeManager",
    "tag.SessionId" : null,
    "tag.Hostname" : "IMPETUS-DSRV03.IMPETUS.CO.IN",
    "MemNonHeapUsedM" : 29.496773,
    "MemNonHeapCommittedM" : 29.75
  }, {
    "name" : "Hadoop:service=NodeManager,name=NodeManagerMetrics",
    "modelerType" : "NodeManagerMetrics",
    "tag.Context" : "yarn",
    "tag.Hostname" : "IMPETUS-DSRV03.IMPETUS.CO.IN",
    "ContainersLaunched" : 0,
    "ContainersCompleted" : 0,
    "ContainersFailed" : 0,
    "ContainersKilled" : 0
  } ]
}
```

The ResourceManager JMX beans

The ResourceManager beans are available at `http://ResourceManagerHost:8088/jmx`. The response is in the JSON format containing an array of various beans objects, such as memory, threads, ResourceManager metrics, and so on.

The following are some of the important beans provided by ResourceManager JMX:

- `ClusterMetrics`: The `ClusterMetrics` of the ResourceManager service contains the ResourceManager's hostname and counts of the NodeManager nodes in the cluster under the `NumActiveNMs`, `NumDecommissionedNMs`, `NumLostNMs`, `NumUnhealthyNMs`, and `NumRebootedNMs` categories.

- `RpcActivity`: This bean provides `RpcActivity` for a port of service. The bean object contains annotated data configured for JMX on that port. For example, port 8031 provides `RegisterNodeManagerNumOps`, `RegisterNodeManagerAvgTime`, `NodeHeartbeatNumOps`, and `NodeHeartbeatAvgTime`.

- `JvmMetrics`: This bean provides the ResourceManager JVM stats for threads, garbage collection, memory, and logging.

- `RMNMInfo`: This bean provides detailed information of the NodeManager associated with the ResourceManager. It consists of a hostname, rack, IPC address, health status, containers, and memory information of all the NodeManager nodes in the cluster.

- `QueueMetrics`: This bean provides the metrics of each queue configured in YARN. For every queue, it provides information regarding applications submitted to the queue, such as `AppsSubmitted`, `AppsRunning`, `AppsPending`, `AppsCompleted`, `AppsKilled`, `AppsFailed`, and the current state of memory, cores, and containers. An interesting section of information is also provided for the running time metrics of the applications in queue. The metrics are provided as `running_0`, `running_60`, `running_300`, and `running_1440`, where `0`, `60`, `300`, and `1440` are time intervals in minutes. It gives the number of applications running over a particular time on the cluster.

- `UgiMetrics`: This bean provides login statistics including `LoginSuccessNumOps`, `LoginSuccessAvgTime`, `LoginFailureNumOps`, and `LoginFailureAvgTime`.

The NodeManager JMX beans

Similar to ResourceManager's JMX data, NodeManager's JMX data is available at `http://NodeManagerHost:8042/jmx`.

The following are some of the important beans provided by NodeManager JMX:

- `JvmMetrics`: Similar to the ResourceManager, this bean provides NodeManager JVM stats for threads, garbage collection, memory, and logging.

- `ShuffleMetrics`: This bean provides shuffle information for the MapReduce applications if configured in the `yarn-site.xml` file. It provides `ShuffleOutputBytes`, `ShuffleOutputsFailed`, `ShuffleOutputsOK`, and `ShuffleConnections` for the configured shuffle service.

- `RpcActivity`: This bean provides `RpcActivity` for a port of service. The bean object contains annotated data configured for JMX on that port. For example, port 8040 provides `RpcQueueTimeNumOps`, `RpcQueueTimeAvgTime`, `RpcAuthenticationFailures`, and `RpcAuthenticationSuccesses`.

- `NodeManagerMetrics`: This bean provides containers details for a particular NameNode service. It includes stats for `ContainersLaunched`, `ContainersCompleted`, `ContainersFailed`, `ContainersKilled`, `ContainersIniting`, `ContainersRunning`, and `AllocatedContainers`.

- `UgiMetrics`: This bean remains the same for both the ResourceManager and NodeManager services and provides login statistics including `LoginSuccessNumOps, LoginSuccessAvgTime, LoginFailureNumOps,` and `LoginFailureAvgTime`

Ganglia monitoring

Ganglia is a scalable and distributed system monitoring tool used to monitor large clusters. It provides memory, CPU usage, and network utilization metrics for all the nodes in a cluster. It provides both live metrics and historical statistics for a certain period of time.

Ganglia uses broadcast and listen protocol for communication and monitoring of services. It uses XML and XRD for data representation and transport. Low per node overheads and high concurrency is achieved using efficient algorithms for gathering the metrics.

Ganglia daemons

Ganglia has a flexible master/slave architectural style with the following two services:

- **Monitoring daemon** (gmond): The monitoring service runs on every node, of the cluster that needs to be monitored by Ganglia. It collects the node as well as the service level metrics, and sends the information to the master daemon.

- **Metadata daemon** (gmetad): The metadata daemon is responsible to collect the data from all the monitoring daemons and create the .rrd files containing the metrics information.

- **Web application**: Ganglia provides a web user-interface for graphical representation of the metrics data. You can view real-time as well as aggregated data through the Ganglia web application.

To install and configure Ganglia, you can refer to the documentation at
http://ganglia.sourceforge.net/.

Integrating Ganglia with Hadoop

Ganglia is used as a tool to monitor metrics of the Hadoop-YARN services. It provides service metrics for the ResourceManager and NodeManager daemons running on a cluster. The Ganglia monitoring daemon reads the JMX data of the YARN services and sends the data to the metadata daemon.

The flexible design of Ganglia allows its daemons to be configured in multiple ways. To make things simple, you can run the Ganglia monitoring daemon (gmond) on all the nodes across the cluster and choose any one node for the Ganglia metadata daemon (gmetad). It is not necessary to run the gmetad daemon node on the master node of the Hadoop-YARN cluster. You can run the metadata daemon on a separate machine as well.

To enable Ganglia monitoring in YARN, an administrator needs to append the following configuration parameters to the hadoop-metrics2.properties file in the configuration directory of the Hadoop-YARN installation (the $HADOOP_PREFIX/etc/hadoop directory), before starting the service:

```
resourcemanager.sink.ganglia.class=org.apache.hadoop.metrics2.sink.
ganglia.GangliaSink31
```

```
resourcemanager.sink.ganglia.servers=centos-server-node1:8649
```

```
resourcemanager.sink.ganglia.period=10
```

```
nodemanager.sink.ganglia.servers=centos-server-node1:8649
```

```
nodemanager.sink.ganglia.class=org.apache.hadoop.metrics2.sink.ganglia.
GangliaSink31
```

```
nodemanager.sink.ganglia.period=10
```

You will find the `.rrd` files with names starting with `yarn.` related to the
ResourceManager and NodeManager services inside the `rrd` directory of the
Ganglia metadata daemon.

Understanding ResourceManager's High Availability

The ResourceManager is a per-cluster service in a YARN cluster. It manages the
cluster resources and schedules the applications on the basis of resource availability.
What if this one service goes down or the node running the services gets out of the
network? The whole cluster would become unusable, as the only point of contact for
the clients is unavailable. Also, the running applications would not be able to acquire
the cluster resources for task execution or status updates.

The ResourceManager service is considered to be the single point of failure in a
cluster. In Hadoop 2.4.1, this issue is resolved and the High Availability feature
of the ResourceManager service is introduced in YARN.

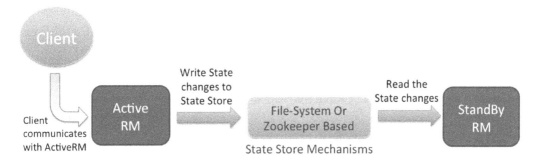

Architecture

A cluster configured with High Availability of ResourceManager has multiple
ResourceManager services running; only one of them is active at a time and the rest
are in standby state. Clients always connect to the active ResourceManager service. It
is important to synchronize the current state of the active ResourceManager service
to all the standby instances.

Currently, YARN defines the following two mechanisms to synchronize the state:

- `FileSystemRMStateStore`
- `ZKRMStateStore`

The `FileSystemRMStateStore` mechanism stores the state using files shared across all the ResourceManager nodes. By default, these files are stored in HDFS.

The Zookeeper-based state store uses a Zookeeper quorum to store the ResourceManager's state. It is a more reliable mechanism than filesystem. It allows only a single ResourceManager service to write to the state store at a time and avoids the split brain scenario (multiple ResourceManager services trying to write to the state store at a given point of time).

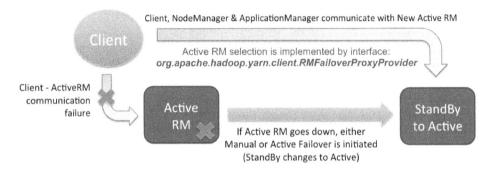

As described in the preceding diagram, when the **Active RM** goes down, the communication between the client and the active RM fails. At that moment, a failover is initiated. A standby ResourceManager service changes to active. All the services, such as RMClient, NodeManager, ApplicationMaster, and so on, that were connecting to the old active RM now connect to the new active RM node. Hadoop-YARN also provides a default mechanism for active RM selection.

Failover mechanisms

Hadoop-YARN provides the following two failover mechanisms for the transition of a standby ResourceManager service to an active state:

- **Manual Failover**: An admin can manually change a ResourceManager service from an active to a standby role, or vice versa. YARN provides a CLI command, `yarn rmadmin`, to manage these transitions. During failover, the admin's manual efforts are needed to transit any one of the standby ResourceManager services to active. The turnaround time for manual failover control depends on the time before the admin comes to know about the issue and the time he/she takes to execute the transition command.

- **Automatic Failover**: In case of automatic failover control, if the active ResourceManager service goes down due to any reason, the standby service will automatically serve requests as active ResourceManager. Similar to High Availability in HDFS, it requires a Zookeeper quorum to initiate failover transition. Although, it does not require a separate process to monitor Zookeeper state like ZKFC in HDFS. The ResourceManager service has an embedded implementation (`ActiveStandbyElector`) for failure detection and Zookeeper leader election.

For production scenarios, it is recommended to configure a Zookeeper quorum for RM state store mechanism over filesystem, and automatic over manual failover.

Configuring ResourceManager's High Availability

By default, the High Availability of the ResourceManager in YARN is disabled. You can enable the `ha` by defining the following property in the `yarn-site.xml` file:

```
<property>
    <name>yarn.resourcemanager.ha.enabled</name>
    <value>true</value>
</property>
```

The configuration of High Availability for the ResourceManager is divided in the following four steps as given in the following figure:

- Define nodes
- The RM state store mechanism
- The failover proxy provider
- Automatic failover (optional, but recommended)

Define nodes

You need to define the ResourceManager ID for hosts and hostnames associated with each ID in the `yarn-site.xml` file:

```
<property>
    <name>yarn.resourcemanager.ha.rm-ids</name>
    <value>rm1,rm2</value>
</property>

<property>
    <name>yarn.resourcemanager.hostname.rm1</name>
    <value>master1</value>
</property>

<property>
    <name>yarn.resourcemanager.hostname.rm2</name>
    <value>master2</value>
</property>
```

You can also explicitly define the ID of the current ResourceManager host by defining the `yarn.resourcemanager.ha.id` property for each ResourceManager host. This is an optional configuration; if not specified, then the ID is figured out by comparing the local address of the RM host and value of the `yarn.resourcemanager.address.{id}` property:

```
<property>
    <name>yarn.resourcemanager.ha.id</name>
    <value>rm1</value>
</property>
```

The RM state store mechanism

You can configure the state store mechanism by configuring the `yarn.resourcemanager.store.class` property in the `yarn-site.xml` file. The default configured mechanism for state store is `org.apache.hadoop.yarn.server.resourcemanager.recovery. FileSystemRMStateStore`.

You need to configure the state store directory, as shown next:

```
<property>
    <name>yarn.resourcemanager.fs.state-store.uri</name>
    <value>hdfs://master:8020/rmstore</value>
</property>
```

The default value for the state store directory is `${hadoop.tmp.dir}/yarn/system/rmstore`.

The directory in the HDFS will be automatically created on ResourceManager startup. Since all the ResourceManager daemons can write to the HDFS directly, there's a possibility for the occurrence of a split brain scenario.

If you need to configure the `ZKRMStateStore` mechanism, you require a Zookeeper quorum already running in your cluster. To install and configure Zookeeper, you can refer to the Apache Zookeeper documentation at `http://zookeeper.apache.org/`.

To configure Zookeeper for the state store mechanism, you need to override the default value with the `ZKRMStateStore` class and define a list of Zookeeper server nodes:

```
<property>
    <name>yarn.resourcemanager.store.class</name>
<value>org.apache.hadoop.yarn.server.resourcemanager.recovery.ZKRM
StateStore</value>
</property>
<property>
    <name>yarn.resourcemanager.zk-address</name>
    <value>zk1:2181,zk2:2181,zk3:2181</value>
</property>
```

`zk-address` is a comma separated list of Zookeeper server nodes defined in the form of `Host:ClientPort`.

The following is a list of configuration properties with their default values for the Zookeeper state store. You can override these values in the `yarn-site.xml` file:

- **Znode for the ResourceManager state store**: You can configure the `znode` path for the Zookeeper ensemble to store the information related to the ResourceManager state store:

```
<property>
    <name>yarn.resourcemanager.zk-state-store.parent-
path</name>
    <value>/rmstore</value>
</property>
```

- **Connection retry count**: The ResourceManager service connects to the Zookeeper ensemble to store the state information. You can configure the number of retry attempts for a ResourceManager to connect to the Zookeeper server:

```
<property>
    <name>yarn.resourcemanager.zk-num-retries</name>
    <value>1000</value>
</property>
```

- **Connection retry interval**: You can configure the interval in milliseconds for retry attempts for a ResourceManager to connect to the Zookeeper server. The default value is `1000` ms:

```
<property>
    <name>yarn.resourcemanager.zk-retry-interval-ms</name>
    <value>1000</value>
</property>
```

To read more about the configuration properties for state store, you can refer to the Apache YARN documentation at `http://hadoop.apache.org/docs/r2.5.1/hadoop-yarn/hadoop-yarn-common/yarn-default.xml`.

The failover proxy provider

The YARN clients, NodeManager daemons, and different ApplicationMasters running in a cluster communicate with the active ResourceManager. During failover, the communication to the active ResourceManager will break and these services need to initialize a new communication interface to the new active ResourceManager daemon.

All these services communicating with the ResourceManager service have a list of configured ResourceManager nodes. They try connecting to ResourceManager in a round-robin way until they successfully connect to one active ResourceManager. If the active ResourceManager goes down, the services start looking for *new* active ResourceManager in the same way until they successfully find another active ResourceManager.

This default implementation of the failover proxy provider is predefined in Hadoop-YARN. If an administrator needs to define a new mechanism, he/she needs to define a class that should implement the `org.apache.hadoop.yarn.client.RMFailoverProxyProvider` interface.

To configure a class for the failover proxy provider, an administrator can define the following property in the `yarn-site.xml` file:

```
<property>
    <name>yarn.client.failover-proxy-provider</name>
<value>org.apache.hadoop.yarn.client.ConfiguredRMFailoverProxyProv
ider</value>
</property>
```

Automatic failover

As mentioned previously, automatic failover is recommended for a production environment and it requires a Zookeeper quorum already running in your cluster. By default, it is enabled and it uses the `zk-address` property defined for the Zookeeper-based state store mechanism:

```
<property>
    <name>yarn.resourcemanager.ha.automatic-
failover.enabled</name>
    <value>true</value>
</property>

<property>
    <name>yarn.resourcemanager.zk-address</name>
    <value>zk1:2181,zk2:2181,zk3:2181</value>
</property>
```

You can also override the value for the `znode` path used for storing leader election information. The default value for the `znode` path is `/yarn-leader-election`:

```
<property>
    <name>yarn.resourcemanager.ha.automatic-failover.zk-base-
path</name>
    <value>/yarn-leader-election</value>
</property>
```

To explore how Zookeeper keeps the leader information and how `znode` works, you can log in to the Zookeeper node and connect to the Zookeeper server using the Zookeeper command line script (`zkCli.sh`).

 You can refer to the Zookeeper documentation at `https://zookeeper.apache.org/doc/r3.4.6/zookeeperStarted.html#sc_ConnectingToZooKeeper`.

High Availability admin commands

ResourceManager High Availability admin commands allow an administrator to configure or query the ResourceManager's state. The following are the important commands available to High Availability admin:

- `yarn rmadmin -transitionToActive rm1`: In case of manual failover control, an administrator runs this command to update the state of the specified ResourceManager as active.

- `yarn rmadmin -transitionToStandby rm1`: Similar to the `transitionToActive` command, an administrator runs this command to update the state of the specified ResourceManager as standby.

- `yarn rmadmin -getServiceState rm1`: Admin can get the status of a particular ResourceManager at any point by executing this command. The output would either be active or standby.

Monitoring NodeManager's health

NodeManager is a per-node daemon running on all the slave nodes of the cluster. All the NodeManager nodes are worker nodes that perform application execution. For efficient scheduling, it is important for the ResourceManager to monitor the health of these nodes. Health may include memory, CPU, network usage, and so on. The ResourceManager daemon will not schedule any new application execution requests to an unhealthy NodeManager.

The health checker script

YARN defines a mechanism to monitor health of a node using a script. An administrator needs to define a shell script to monitor the node. If the script returns ERROR as the first word in any of the output lines, then the ResourceManager marks the node as UNHEALTHY.

A sample script to check the memory usage of a node is written next. It checks the current memory usage and if the memory usage is greater than 95%, it prints an error message. You need to create a shell script such as `check_memory_usage.sh` and change its permissions to allow the execution of permissions.

A sample NodeManager health check script:

```
#!/bin/bash
mem_usage=$(echo `free -m | awk '/^Mem/ {printf("%u", 100*$3/$2);}'`)
echo "Usage is $mem_usage%"
```

```
if [ $mem_usage -ge 95 ]
    then
    echo 'ERROR: Memory Usage is greater than 95%'
    else
    echo 'NORMAL: Memory Usage is less than 95%'
fi
```

You need to configure the path of the health script and runtime arguments required to run the script (if any) in the `yarn-site.xml` file by using the following properties:

```
<property>
    <name>yarn.nodemanager.health-checker.script.path</name>
    <value>/home/hduser/check_memory_usage.sh</value>
</property>

<property>
    <name>yarn.nodemanager.health-checker.script.opts</name>
    <value>arg1 arg2</value>
</property>
```

The sample script mentioned previously does not require any runtime arguments.

If the output of the above mentioned sample script is `ERROR: Memory Usage is greater than 95%`, then the ResourceManager updates the state of the NodeManager to `UNHEALTHY`.

Some optional health checker properties defined in `yarn-default.xml` are mentioned next. You can override these properties in the `yarn-site.xml` file.

```
<property>
    <name>yarn.nodemanager.health-checker.interval-ms</name>
    <value>600000</value>
    <description>Frequency of running node health
script</description>
</property>

<property>
    <name>yarn.nodemanager.health-checker.script.timeout-ms</name>
    <value>1200000</value>
    <description>Script time out period</description>
</property>
```

To view the list of unhealthy nodes in the cluster, you can browse to the ResourceManager web UI at `http://ResourceManagerHost:8088/cluster/nodes/unhealthy`.

Summary

In this chapter, we covered the Hadoop-YARN command line interface, that is, the usage of the user, as well as administrative commands. You can now use the different Hadoop-YARN scripts to start or stop services with ease and read log files wherever required. We also talked about the configurations related to different components and the list of default ports used by each component.

With the help of monitoring tools and JMX data, you can analyze cluster state and performance. Features such as recovery, High Availability, and health script checker are now supported.

The next chapter will talk about application execution over a YARN cluster. It gives an in-depth explanation of the application execution phases with the help of a sample MapReduce application.

4
Executing Applications Using YARN

YARN is used to manage resources and execute different applications over a multi-node cluster. It allows users to submit any type of application to the cluster. It solves scalability and MapReduce framework-related issues by providing a generic implementation of application execution.

This chapter targets the YARN users and developers to develop their understanding of the application execution flow. With the help of flow diagrams and snapshots, it explains how the YARN components communicate with each other during application execution.

In this chapter, we'll cover:

- Understanding application execution flow
- Submitting a sample MapReduce application
- Handling failures in YARN
- Exploring container and application logs

Understanding application execution flow

A YARN application can be a simple shell script, MapReduce job, or any group of jobs. This section will cover YARN application submission and execution flow. To manage application execution over YARN, a client needs to define an ApplicationMaster. The client submits an application context to the ResourceManager. As per the application needs, the ResourceManager then allocates memory for an ApplicationMaster and containers for application execution.

The complete process of application execution can be broadly divided into six phases, as shown in the following figure:

Phase 1 – Application initialization and submission

In the first phase of application execution, a client will connect to the applications manager service of the ResourceManager daemon and will request the ResourceManager for a new application ID. The ResourceManager will validate the client request and if the client is an authorized user, it will send a new and unique application ID, along with the cluster metrics to the client. The client will use this application ID, and will submit an application to the ResourceManager as described in the following figure:

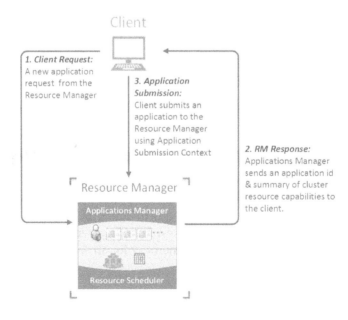

The client will send `ApplicationSubmissionContext` along with the submission request. The submission context contains metadata information related to an application, such as application queue, name, and so on. It also contains the information to start the ApplicationMaster service on a particular node. The application submission is a blocking call which waits for the application completion. In the background, the ResourceManager service will accept the application and will allocate containers for application execution.

Phase 2 – Allocate memory and start ApplicationMaster

In the second phase, the ResourceManager daemon starts an ApplicationMaster service on any of the NodeManager node. The scheduler service within the ResourceManager is responsible for the node selection. The basic criteria for selecting a node for the ApplicationMaster container is that the amount of memory required by the ApplicationMaster service should be available on that node. This is shown in the following figure:

The ApplicationSubmissionContext submitted by the client contains LaunchContext for the ApplicationMaster's container. The LaunchContext contains information such as the memory requirements for ApplicationMaster, command to start the ApplicationMaster, and so on.

The scheduler service of the ResourceManager daemon allocates memory specified in the `LaunchContext` and sends the context a NodeManager node to start the ApplicationMaster service.

Phase 3 – ApplicationMaster registration and resource allocation

ApplicationMaster's container creates clients to communicate with the ResourceManager and NodeManager of the cluster. The ApplicationMaster then registers itself with the ResourceManager using the AMRMClient service. It specifies the host and port for the container it is running on. While developing an application, a developer can also use AMRMClientAsync, an asynchronous implementation of the AppMaster ResourceManager client.

It also sends a tracking URL for the application. The tracking URL is an application specific framework used to monitor the application execution.

The ResourceManager sends back the registration response with information related to access control lists, cluster capabilities, and access tokens, as shown in the following figure:

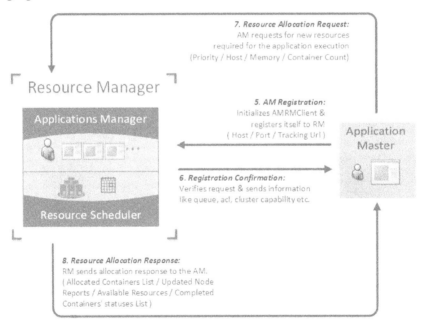

The ApplicationMaster requests the ResourceManager for containers allocation on the NodeManager nodes to execute the application tasks. The request includes the desired capabilities of the worker containers in terms of memory and CPU cores with the application priority. The optional parameters include nodes and racks specifications for execution of containers.

The ResourceManager iterates the list of asked containers, filters out the blacklisted containers, and creates a list of containers to be released.

Phase 4 – Launch and monitor containers

Once the ResourceManager allocates the requested containers to the ApplicationMaster, the ApplicationMaster connects to the NodeManager nodes using AMNMClient. The ApplicationMaster sends the LaunchContext for each worker container to the NodeManager node. It is also possible that the ResourceManager allocates two containers on a single NodeManager node. The NodeManager node then uses the information in the LaunchContext to start a container. Each container runs as a YARN child process on the NodeManager node.

The ApplicationMaster asks for the status of the current state of running containers. The response for container status request consists of a list of newly created and completed container's information, as described in the following figure:

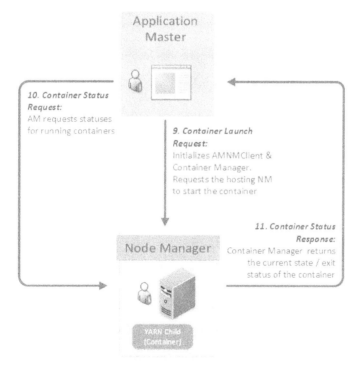

For all the containers, the ResourceManager performs the following actions:

- Liveliness check on the ApplicationMaster
- Updates the asked / released / blacklisted containers' list
- Validates the new resource requirements, allocates resources, and updates the cluster resource metrics

Phase 5 – Application progress report

An application specific framework to monitor the application is exposed through the tracking URL for that application. The YARN client uses the tracking URL to monitor the current status of an application. The tracking URL generally contains the application metrics. For example, if the application is a MapReduce job, then the tracking URL will expose the list of mappers and reducers for the job, as described in the following figure:

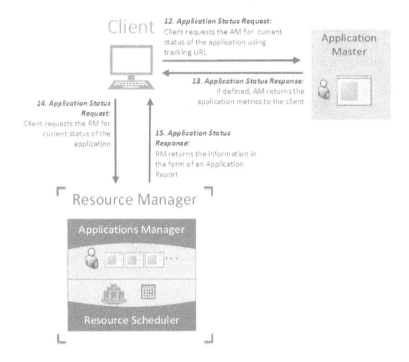

At any point in time, the YARN client may request the applications manager service of the ResourceManager to get the status of an application. The ResourceManager sends the application status in the form of an application report.

Phase 6 – Application completion

On completion of an application, the ApplicationMaster sends out an un-registration request to the ResourceManager. The ApplicationMaster terminates itself and releases the used memory back to the NodeManager. For an application, there is a final state and a final status. The ResourceManager marks the final state of the application as FINISHED. The final status of the application is set by the ApplicationMaster and is specific to the application executed.

The YARN client may interrupt the application execution at any point by sending a kill request to the ResourceManager. The ResourceManager kills the running containers for that application and changes the application status to completed.

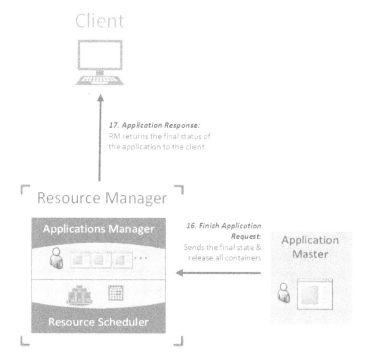

Submitting a sample MapReduce application

When a MapReduce application is submitted to a Hadoop-YARN cluster, a series of events occurs in different components. In this section, we will submit a sample Hadoop-YARN application to a cluster. We will discuss the application flow with the help of snapshots and understand how the series of events occurs.

Submitting an application to the cluster

As discussed in *Chapter 3, Administering a Hadoop-YARN Cluster*, the `yarn jar` command is used to submit a MapReduce application to a Hadoop-YARN cluster. An example `jar` is packaged inside the Hadoop bundle. It contains sample MapReduce programs, such as word count, pi estimator, pattern search, and so on. This is shown in the following figure:

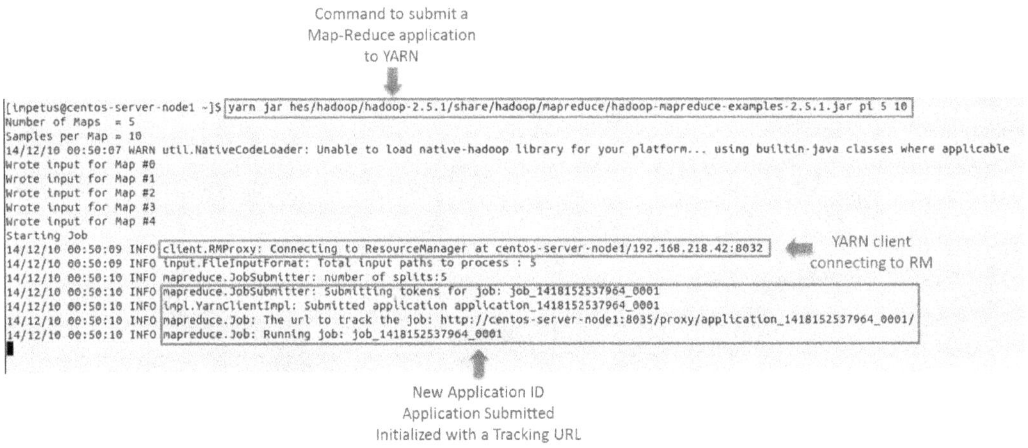

As shown in the preceding diagram, we have submitted a `pi` job with 5 and 10 as sample arguments. The first argument 5 denotes the number of map tasks and the second argument 10 represents the samples per map as parameters to the job.

```
yarn jar <jarPath> <JobName> <arguments>
```

Connect to a Hadoop master node and execute the command as specified in the diagram. Once the job is submitted, the command reads the configuration files and creates a connection to the ResourceManager. It uses the ResourceManager host and RPC port specified in the `yarn-site.xml` file. The ResourceManager registers the request and provides a unique ID to the application. The application ID is prefixed with `application_` to the ID provided by the ResourceManager. For the MapReduce jobs, a job ID prefixed with `job_` is also created.

The ResourceManager accepts the application and starts an MRApplicationMaster service on one of the nodes to manage the application execution. The ApplicationMaster then registers itself to the ResourceManager. After successful registration, a tracking URL is provided to track the status of the application and progress of the different containers executed for that application.

Updates in the ResourceManager web UI

Once the application is successfully submitted and accepted by the ResourceManager, the cluster's resource metrics are updated and application progress is visible on the ResourceManager web interface. This is shown in the following screenshot:

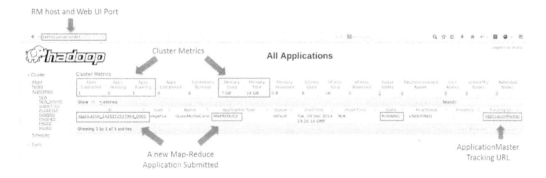

The HTTP web interface is available at the ResourceManager hostname and port specified against the `yarn.resourcemanager.webapp.address` property in the `yarn-site.xml` file.

You can browse to the ResourceManager URL from your master node at `http://localhost:8088/`

Also, if you are using a multi-node Hadoop-YARN cluster, then replace the localhost with the actual ResourceManager hostname.

The landing page contains a summary of the cluster metrics and a list containing all the applications for the cluster. It also contains metadata about the application, such as the current state, application name, and so on. The web interface also contains information related to the NodeManager nodes and available queues.

Understanding the application process

In the first step, when an application is submitted to a Hadoop-YARN cluster, the RunJar class is instantiated. The RunJar class is a java process that is used as an interface between the client and the ResourceManager node. This is shown in the following figure:

To check for all the Java processes running on the system, the jps command is used. The output of the jps command on the client node will contain a process named as RunJar. The output will also contain the process ID for all the java processes.

To see the process information, you can use the ps aux command. It lists all the processes running on the node. To filter out the result, you can use the grep command along with the process ID. The command will look as shown next:

```
ps aux | grep <processID>
```

Tracking application details

The ResourceManager web interface provides application details at
`http://<RMHost>:<WebPort>/http://<RMHost>:<WebPort>/cluster/apps/<application_id>`

The ResourceManager web interface provides generic information about the applications submitted to it. This is shown in the following figure:

For each application, there can be multiple attempts on the same or different nodes. The application details page contains the list of nodes used for every attempt of application execution. It provides links for the log files generated for the application.

The ApplicationMaster process

An ApplicationMaster is a first container for an application. Every application framework has a predefined ApplicationMaster to manage the application execution. To manage the MapReduce application execution, Hadoop is bundled with the MRAppMaster service. This is shown in the following screenshot:

```
[inpetus@centos-server-node1 ~]$ jps
24172 NameNode
5243 RunJar
5844 YarnChild
24411 NodeManager
24460 WebAppProxyServer
5830 YarnChild
5822 YarnChild
5834 YarnChild
5850 YarnChild
24255 DataNode
74356 ResourceManager
5938 Jps
5533 MRAppMaster
5054 YarnChild
[inpetus@centos-server-node1 ~]$ ps aux | grep 5533
inpetus   5533 28.1  6.7 1621500 137758 ?       Sl   01:02   0:08 /usr/lib/jvm/jdk1.7.0_21//bin/java -Dlog4j.configuration=container-log4j.properties -Dyarn.app.container.log.dir=/home/inpetus/hes/hadoop/ha
doop-2.5.1/logs/userlogs/application_1418152537964_0005/container_1418152537964_0005_01_000001 -Dyarn.app.container.log.filesize=0 -Dhadoop.root.logger=INFO,CLA -Xmx1024m org.apache.hadoop.mapreduce.v2.app
.MRAppMaster
inpetus   5996  0.0  0.0 103244   872 pts/2    S+   01:02   0:00 grep 5533
[inpetus@centos-server-node1 ~]$
```

The MRApplicationMaster for MapReduce applications runs as a Java process. The name of the process is MRAppMaster. Similar to the RunJar process, you can execute the jps and ps aux commands on the node running the MRApplicationMaster service.

Cluster nodes information

The ResourceManager web interface provides the nodes list at
`http://<RMHost>:<WebPort>/cluster/nodes`. This is shown in the
following screenshot:

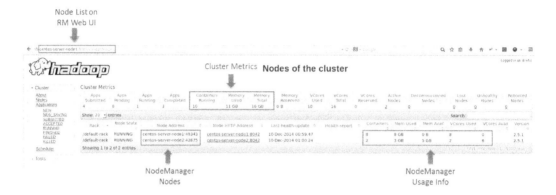

It provides the list of the NodeManager nodes. The node metadata includes the rack
name, current state, RPC and HTTP addresses, and node capability metrics. It also
contains cluster metrics similar to the metrics available on the application list page.
You may notice that the node usage is updated as the job progresses.

Node's container list

All the NodeManager daemons provide a web interface to monitor the containers
running on the node. The address for the NodeManager web interface is

`http://<NMHost>:<WebPort>/node.`

The default value of port for the NodeManager web interface is `8042` as shown in the
following screenshot:

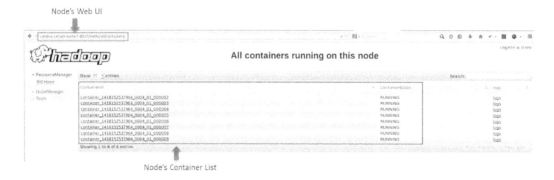

The details of all the containers currently running on a NodeManager node is available at `http://<NMHost>:<WebPort>/http://<NMHost>:<WebPort>/node/allContainers`.

It provides current state of the containers and a link to the logs generated by the container.

YARN child processes

Containers are considered as the worker services. The actual MapReduce tasks are executed inside these containers. Containers in a Hadoop-YARN cluster run as a `YarnChild` Java process. Each MapReduce task will be executed as `YarnChild` and a node can have multiple `YarnChild` processes running simultaneously, as shown in the following:

```
[impetus@centos-server-node1 ~]$ jps
6298 YarnChild
6313 YarnChild
24172 NameNode
5243 RunJar
24411 NodeManager
24469 WebAppProxyServer
6393 Jps
6122 YarnChild
6291 YarnChild
24255 DataNode
24356 ResourceManager
6311 YarnChild
5533 MRAppMaster
6309 YarnChild
[impetus@centos-server-node1 ~]$ ps aux | grep 6298
impetus   6298 14.9  4.7 703632 97272 ?     Sl   01:02   0:03 /usr/lib/jvm/jdk1.7.0_21/jbin/java -Djava.net.preferIPv4Stack=true -Dhadoop.metrics.log.level=WARN -Xmx200m -Djava.io.tmpdir=/home/impetus/h
es/hadoopdirs/hadooptmp/nm-local-dir/usercache/impetus/appcache/application_1418152537964_0005/container_1418152537964_0005_01_000022/tmp -Dlog4j.configuration=container-log4j.properties -Dyarn.app.contain
er.log.dir=/home/impetus/hes/hadoop/hadoop-2.5.1/logs/userlogs/application_1418152537964_0005/container_1418152537964_0005_01_000022 -Dyarn.app.container.log.filesize=0 -Dhadoop.root.logger=INFO,CLA org.ap
ache.hadoop.mapred.YarnChild 192.168.218.42 46550 attempt_1418152537964_0005_m_000019_0 22
impetus   6433  0.0  0.0 103240   872 pts/2     S+   01:03   0:00 grep 6298
[impetus@centos-server-node1 ~]$
```

Similar to the `RunJar` and `MRAppMaster` processes, you can execute the `jps` and `ps aux` commands on the node running the MapReduce tasks.

Application details after completion

Once the MapReduce application is finished, the state and the final status for the application are updated. The tracking URL also gets updated to a link for the application specific history server. We'll discuss the history server further in *Chapter 6, Migrating from MRv1 to MRv2.*

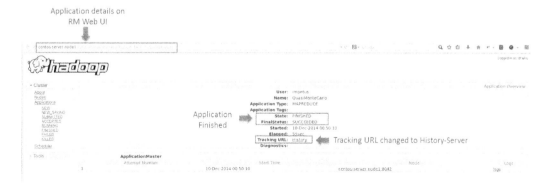

Handling failures in YARN

A successful execution of a YARN application depends on robust coordination of all the YARN components, including containers, ApplicationMaster, NodeManager, and ResourceManager. Any fault in the coordination of the components or lack of sufficient cluster resource can cause the application to fail. The YARN framework is robust in terms of handling failures at different stages in the application execution path. The fault tolerance and recovery of the application depends on its current stage of execution and the component in which the problem occurs. The following section explains the recovery mechanism applied by YARN at component level.

The container failure

Containers are instantiated for executing the map or reduce tasks. As mentioned in the previous section, these containers in Hadoop-YARN are Java processes running as YarnChild processes. There could be some exception in the execution or abnormal termination of JVM due to lack of sufficient resources. The failure is either propagated back from the container to the ApplicationMaster, or the ApplicationMaster notices it when it doesn't receive any response from a container over a period of time (the timeout is set by the property `mapreduce.task.timeout`). In both the scenarios, the task attempt is marked as failed.

The ApplicationMaster then tries to reschedule or re-execute the task and only after a specific number of task attempts are failed, is the complete task considered as failed. The max number of retries is configured by `mapreduce.map.maxattempts` for map tasks and `mapreduce.reduce.maxattempts` for reduce tasks. A job is considered as failed if a certain percent age of map or reduce tasks are failed during the job execution. The percentage is configured by the `mapreduce.map.failures.maxpercent` and `mapreduce.reduce.failures.maxpercent` properties for mappers and reducers respectively.

The ApplicationMaster manages the application execution and containers running. There is always only one instance of ApplicationMaster running for an application. The ApplicationMaster sends a heartbeat to the ResourceManager daemon periodically. In case of ApplicationManager failure, the ResourceManager would not receive any heartbeat within the specified time interval and would then consider the ApplicationMaster a failure. You can also configure the expiry interval for an ApplicationMaster reporting by configuring the `yarn.am.liveness-monitor.expiry-interval-ms` property in the `yarn-site.xml` file.

An application can have multiple attempts on failure. An attempt is marked as failed if the ApplicationMaster fails in between the application execution. The maximum retry attempt count for application execution is configured using the `yarn.resourcemanager.am.max-retries` property. By default, the value is `2` and the preceding property is a global setting for all the ApplicationMasters in the cluster. This value is considered as the upper bound defined for the cluster. An ApplicationMaster can specify its maximum retry count, but the individual count cannot be more than the specified global upper bound.

The NodeManager failure

The NodeManager daemon keeps on periodically sending the liveliness heartbeat to the ResourceManager. The ResourceManager maintains a list of the active NodeManager nodes. If a NodeManager fails, the ResourceManager waits for a heartbeat for the specified time interval. The ResourceManager wait time interval is configured by setting up the value in millisecond for property `yarn.resourcemanager.nm.liveness-monitor.expiry-interval-ms`. Its default value is `600000` (10 minutes). The ResourceManager removes the node information from the active node list and marks the node as a `Lost` node.

An MRApplicationMaster can blacklist a NodeManager node. If a task fails on a particular node for a number of times, the ApplicationMaster will mark the node as blacklisted. You can configure the maximum retry count allowed for a node using the `mapreduce.job.maxtaskfailures.per.tracker` property. Its default value is `3`, which means that if more than `3` tasks fails on a NodeManager, then the ApplicationMaster will mark the node as a blacklisted node and will schedule the tasks on a different node.

The ResourceManager failure

Before Hadoop 2.4.1 release, the ResourceManager was the single point of failure in a Hadoop-YARN cluster. With Hadoop-2.4.1, manual as well as automatic failover control is achieved for high availability of the ResourceManager. A detailed explanation of high availability and its implementation is provided in *Chapter 3, Administering a Hadoop-YARN Cluster*. An administrator can also enable the ResourceManager recovery to handle a failure scenario. By default, the recovery is disabled and you can enable the recovery by setting the `yarn.resourcemanager.recovery.enabled` property to `true`.

If the recovery is enabled, you need to configure a state-store mechanism to store the ResourceManager information. To read more about the state-store mechanisms available, you can refer to the ResourceManager High Availability or the apache documentation at `http://hadoop.apache.org/docs/r2.5.1/hadoop-yarn/hadoop-yarn-site/ResourceManagerRestart.html`.

YARN application logging

With the execution of an application over a YARN cluster, logs are generated for activities in the different components. These logs are broadly classified as follows:

Services logs

The ResourceManager and NodeManager daemons run 24 x 7 on the cluster nodes. These services keep a track of the activities on the cluster and coordinate with the other processes such as ApplicationMaster and container. The YARN service logs are created under the logs directory in the HADOOP_PREFIX directory. You can refer to the managing service logs section in the previous chapter.

Application logs

The ApplicationMaster, as well as the containers running in the cluster, generate the application logs. Logging allows the debugging and analyzing of applications. By default, these logs are generated under the user_logs directory of logs in the Hadoop installation folder. You can configure the location of the directory by using the following property:

```
<property>
    <name>yarn.nodemanager.log-dirs</name>
    <value>/home/hduser/hadoop-2.5.1/logs/yarn</value>
<property>
```

An application running over YARN is provided with a unique ID. The container's ID is derived from the application ID by appending the container number to it. The logs for an application are generated in the directory with application ID containing directories of the containers logs named with containers ID.

Each container generates the following three log types:

- stderr: This file contains the error that occurred during the execution of the particular container.

- syslog: This file contains the log messages for the configured log level. Default logging is done for INFO, WARN ERROR, and FATAL log messages.

- stdout: This file contains the print messages encountered in the container execution flow.

The three logs are shown in the following screenshot:

Logs for
container_1414205634577_0001_01_000001

- ResourceManager
  RM Home
- NodeManager
- Tools

stderr : Total file length is 222 bytes.
stdout : Total file length is 0 bytes.
syslog : Total file length is 70016 bytes.

Summary

This chapter showcased how an application is executed over a YARN cluster. The chapter started with explaining the phases involved in the execution flow for an application. These phases explicate the coordination and communication happening between the different YARN components during application execution.

We executed a sample application provided by Hadoop over the YARN cluster. For the sample application, we saw how an application is submitted to the ResourceManager and how YARN executes the containers of the application as a YarnChild process over the cluster nodes. We also covered progress reports and resource utilization through the ResourceManager web UI.

We also discussed the different failure scenarios and a brief overview about logging in YARN. This chapter was intended to help the users in debugging and analyzing the flow of applications submitted to the cluster.

In the next chapter, we will discuss the internal life cycle management in YARN. It is an extension of the application execution flow and it will cover the state management in detail.

5
Understanding YARN Life Cycle Management

The YARN framework consists of ResourceManager and NodeManager services. These services maintain different components of the life cycle associated with YARN such as an application, a container, a resource, and so on. This chapter focuses on the core implementation of YARN framework and describes how ResourceManager and NodeManager manage the application execution in a distributed environment.

It does not matter if you are a Java developer, an open source contributor, a cluster administrator, or a user; this chapter provides a simple and easy approach to gain YARN insights. In this chapter, we'll discuss the following topics:

- Introduction to state management analogy
- ResourceManager's view for a node, an application, an application attempt, and a container
- NodeManager's view for an application, a container, and a resource
- Analyzing transitions through logs

An introduction to state management analogy

Life cycle is an important phenomenon in event-driven implementation of components in any system. Components of the system pass through a predefined series of valid states. The transition across states is governed by events associated with the state and actions to be performed to address the event occurred.

Here are the some key terms that are used in this chapter:

- **State**: In computer science, the state of a computer program is a technical term for all the stored information, at a given instance in time, to which the program has access.

- **Event**: An event is an action or occurrence detected by the program that may be handled by the program. Typically, events are handled synchronously with the program flow, that is, the program has one or more dedicated places where events are handled.

- **Event handle**: Handles are associated with the events that describe what would be the next state and store information for the process if a particular event occurred.

- **State transition**: This is defined as transition of a state and change in stored information of the process based on the occurrence of an event.

The state of processes such as an ApplicationMaster, a container, and so on, is the information stored in the process is helpful for YARN services for initializing and monitoring the complete execution of the applications or tasks. The key decisions, such as application initialization, resource scheduling and allocation, application termination, releasing resources, and so on, are handled with the help of state transitions and event handlers. When an event occurs, the state of the corresponding component is changed, the state information is updated, and an event handle is executed based on the event.

Let's make it simple with the help of an example. The ResourceManager service stores information for the NodeManager services running across the cluster. The information contains details of the NodeManager service, including the current state of the NodeManager. If the NodeManager service is up, the state of NodeManager is **RUNNING**. When an event to decommission a node is triggered, then the state of the NodeManager service is updated to **DECOMMISSIONED**.

In this chapter, we'll cover such scenarios and discuss how ResourceManager and NodeManager services maintain a life cycle for YARN processes. This chapter will focus on the different views for the ResourceManager and NodeManager services. Each view will have the following:

- **Enumeration definitions**: This defines the different events and states.

- **List of classes involved**: This defines the implementation of event handlers and state transitions. The execution of the event handle updates the information of the process associated with the view in the cluster metrics.

- **State transition diagram**: This explains the state transitions with a flow diagram. A transition diagram will have a start state and a few final states.

The ResourceManager's view

Being the master service, the ResourceManager service manages the following:

- Cluster resources (nodes in the cluster)
- Applications submitted to the cluster
- Attempt of running applications
- Containers running on cluster nodes

The ResourceManager service has its own view for different processes associated with YARN management and application execution of YARN. The following is the view of ResourceManager:

- **Node**: This is the machine with the NodeManager daemon
- **Application**: This is the code submitted by any client to the ResourceManager
- **Application attempt**: This attempt is associated with the execution of any application
- **Container**: This is the process running the business logic of the submitted application

View 1 – Node

The node view of ResourceManager manages the life cycle for NodeManager nodes within a cluster. For every node in the cluster, the ResourceManager maintains an `RMNode` object. The states and event types of a node are defined in enumerations `NodeState` and `RMNodeEventType`.

Here is the list of enumerations and classes involved:

- `org.apache.hadoop.yarn.server.resourcemanager.rmnode.RMNode`: This is an interface to a NodeManager's information on available resources such as its capability, applications executed, running containers, and so on.
- `org.apache.hadoop.yarn.server.resourcemanager.rmnode.RMNodeImpl`: This is used to keep track of all the applications/containers running on a node and defines node state transitions.
- `org.apache.hadoop.yarn.server.resourcemanager.rmnode.RMNodeEventType`: This is an enumeration that defines different event types for a node.
- `org.apache.hadoop.yarn.api.records.NodeState`: This is an enumeration that defines different states of a node.

The following state transition diagram explains the ResourceManager's view of a node:

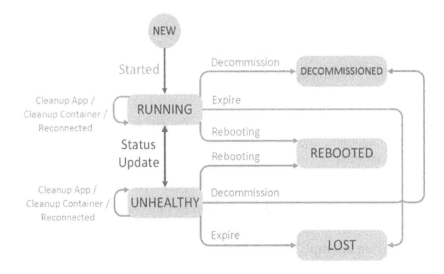

The start and final states of the ResourceManager's view of a node are as follows:

- Start state: **NEW**
- Final states: **DECOMMISSION / REBOOTED / LOST**

As soon as a NodeManager registers itself to the ResourceManager, the node is marked with the **NEW** state. The state is updated to **RUNNING** after successful registration. An AddNodeTransition event handler is initiated, which updates the scheduler with the new node and its capabilities. If the node already exists in the inactive RM nodes list, it removes the node from the inactive list and updates the cluster metrics with rejoined node information. If the node is new, it directly increments the active node count in the cluster metrics.

Every NodeManager daemon sends its liveliness information as a heartbeat to the ResourceManager. ResourceManager keeps track of each node's last heartbeat, and the nodes with the last contact value greater than the configured value specified for the cluster are considered as expired nodes. By default, the time to wait until a NodeManager is considered dead is 600000 ms, that is, 10 minutes. The node is marked as **UNUSABLE** and is added to the inactive node list of the ResourceManager. All the containers running on a dead node are assumed to be dead and new containers will be scheduled to other NodeManager daemons. A NodeManager can also be decommissioned from the cluster or be rebooted due to technical reasons.

The heartbeat of the NodeManager also contains information related to the running or finished containers on that node. If the node is healthy, the node information is updated with latest metrics and initiates a node update scheduler event for the next heartbeat. The ResourceManager also keeps track of completed applications and containers for every NodeManager.

In case of a reboot or restart of service, a NodeManager tries to reconnect to the ResourceManager to resume its services. If the reconnected node's configuration (the total capability and the HTTP port of node) differs, the NodeManager replaces the old or resets the heartbeat if the reconnected node is the same. The scheduler is updated with a new node added event and the node is marked as RUNNING.

The NodeHealthCheckerService class defined in the package for YARN NodeManager determines the health of a node. Every node performs a health checkup by periodically running a script on the node configured by the yarn. nodemanager.health-checker.script.path property in the yarn configuration file. The default frequency of running the node health script is 600000 ms, that is, 10 minutes, and is configured using the yarn.nodemanager.health-checker. interval-ms property.

The NodeHealthScriptRunner class runs the health check-up script on the node, parses the output from the node health monitor script and checks for the presence of error pattern in the report. The timed out script or script, which causes the IOException output is ignored. If the script throws java.io.IOException or org. apache.hadoop.util.Shell.ExitCodeException, the output is ignored and the node is left remaining healthy, as a script might have a syntax error.

The node is marked unhealthy if:

- The node health script times out
- The node health scripts output has a line, which begins with ERROR
- An exception is thrown while executing the script

The node also runs a DiskHealthCheckerService class, to get the disks' health information of the node. To read more about the node health checker script, you can refer to *Chapter 3, Administering a Hadoop-YARN Cluster*.

Here is a summarized table view for ResourceManager's view of a node:

Current State	Event Occurred	New State	Event Class Instantiated
NEW	STARTED	**RUNNING**	AddNodeTransition
RUNNING	STATUS_UPDATE	**RUNNING / UNHEALTHY**	StatusUpdateWhenHealthy Transition
	CLEANUP_APP	**RUNNING**	CleanUpAppTransition
	CLEANUP_ CONTAINER	**RUNNING**	CleanUpContainerTransition
	RECONNECTED	**RUNNING**	ReconnectNodeTransition
	DECOMMISSION	**DECOMMISSIONED**	DeactivateNodeTransition
	EXPIRE	**LOST**	DeactivateNodeTransition
	REBOOTING	**REBOOTED**	DeactivateNodeTransition
UNHEALTHY	STATUS_UPDATE	**RUNNING / UNHEALTHY**	StatusUpdateWhenUnHealthy Transition
	CLEANUP_APP	**UNHEALTHY**	CleanUpAppTransition
	CLEANUP_ CONTAINER	**UNHEALTHY**	CleanUpContainerTransition
	RECONNECTED	**UNHEALTHY**	ReconnectNodeTransition
	DECOMMISSION	**DECOMMISSIONED**	DeactivateNodeTransition
	EXPIRE	**LOST**	DeactivateNodeTransition
	REBOOTING	**REBOOTED**	DeactivateNodeTransition

View 2 – Application

The application view of ResourceManager represents the application's life cycle managed by ResourceManager during the application's execution over the YARN cluster. In the previous chapter, we discussed the different phases related to application execution. This section will give you a more detailed explanation on how ResourceManager handles an application life cycle.

Here is the list of enumerations and classes involved:

- `org.apache.hadoop.yarn.server.resourcemanager.rmapp.RMApp`: This is an interface to an application for the ResourceManager

- `org.apache.hadoop.yarn.server.resourcemanager.rmapp.RMAppImpl`: This is used to access various updates in application status/report and defines application state transitions

- `org.apache.hadoop.yarn.server.resourcemanager.rmapp.RMAppEventType`: This is an enumeration defining the different event types for an application

- `org.apache.hadoop.yarn.server.resourcemanager.rmapp.RMAppState`: This is an enumeration defining the different states of an application

The following state transition diagram explains the ResourceManager's view of an application:

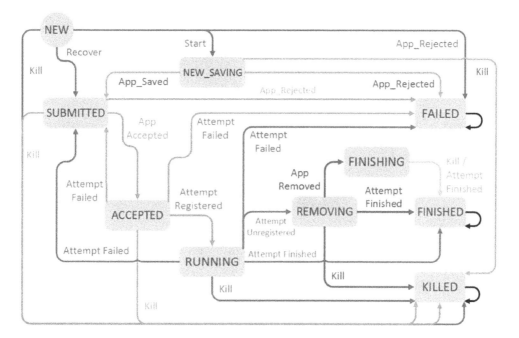

The start and final states of the ResourceManager's view of an application are as follows:

- Start state: **NEW**
- Final states: **FAILED / FINISHED / KILLED**

When a client submits a new application request to ResourceManager, RM registers the application and provides a unique application ID. (Phase 1 for application execution flow in the previous chapter). The application state is initialized with **NEW**.

The `RMAppImpl` object maintains a set of `RMNode` objects that contain the information related to the current state of a node. During a `NODE_UPDATE` event, the ResourceManager updates the information for usable and unusable nodes in the cluster. The state of an application in the **NEW** state is unchanged during the `NODE_UPDATE` event.

The client submits the application using application submission content. If recovery of ResourceManager is enabled, the submission context for an application is stored in the configured state store for ResourceManager. Once the application context is saved, it is submitted to the cluster, which means it is being put in a queue for execution.

The applications are picked up for execution from the configured queues; if the resource requirement of an application is met, then the application will be accepted and its state changes to **ACCEPTED**.

An `App_Rejected` event is triggered if the application is rejected due to insufficient resources or some exception. In this case, the application will be marked as **FAILED**.

ApplicationMaster is launched as the first attempt of the application execution on one of the nodes. ApplicationMaster will register its attempt with ResourceManager and create an `RMAppAttempt` context for that attempt. After successful registration, the state of the application will be changed to **RUNNING**.

On successful completion, the application attempt first unregisters its attempt, changes the state to **REMOVING**, and then it moves to the **FINISHED** state. An attempt can directly move from **RUNNING** to **FINISHED** state if it is an unmanaged attempt.

If an attempt fails, the ResourceManager will re-execute the application attempt on another node. The application is marked as **SUBMITTED** with the trigger of the `Attempt_Failed` event and it increments the applications attempt count. If the retry count exceeds the maximum retry count specified in the configuration, the application will be marked as **FAILED**.

You can configure the number of maximum attempts allowed for an application in `yarn-site.xml` as follows:

```
<property>
    <description>Default value is 2</description>
    <name>yarn.resourcemanager.am.max-attempts</name>
    <value>2</value>
</property>
```

At any state of application, including **SUBMITTED**, **ACCEPTED**, **RUNNING**, and so on, if a kill signal or event is sent by the user, the state of the application will be directly updated to the **KILLED** state and all the containers used by the application will be released.

Here is a summarized table view for ResourceManager's view of an application:

Current State	Event Occurred	New State	Event Class Instantiated
NEW	NODE_UPDATE	**NEW**	RMAppNodeUpdateTransition
	START	**NEW_SAVING**	RMAppNewlySavingTransition
	RECOVER	**SUBMITTED**	StartAppAttemptTransition
	KILL	**KILLED**	AppKilledTransition
	APP_REJECTED	**FAILED**	AppRejectedTransition
NEW_SAVING	NODE_UPDATE	**NEW_SAVING**	RMAppNodeUpdateTransition
	APP_SAVED	**SUBMITTED**	StartAppAttemptTransition
	KILL	**KILLED**	AppKilledTransition
	APP_REJECTED	**FAILED**	AppRejectedTransition
SUBMITTED	NODE_UPDATE	**SUBMITTED**	RMAppNodeUpdateTransition
	APP_REJECTED	**FAILED**	AppRejectedTransition
	APP_ACCEPTED	**ACCEPTED**	
	KILL	**KILLED**	KillAppAndAttemptTransition

Current State	Event Occurred	New State	Event Class Instantiated
ACCEPTED	NODE_UPDATE	**ACCEPTED**	RMAppNodeUpdateTransition
	ATTEMPT_ REGISTERED	**RUNNING**	
	ATTEMPT_FAILED	**SUBMITTED, FAILED**	AttemptFailedTransition
	KILL	**KILLED**	KillAppAndAttemptTransition
RUNNING	NODE_UPDATE	**RUNNING**	RMAppNodeUpdateTransition
	ATTEMPT_ UNREGISTERED	**REMOVING**	RMAppRemovingTransition
	ATTEMPT_FINISHED	**FINISHED**	FINISHED_TRANSITION
	ATTEMPT_FAILED	**SUBMITTED, FAILED**	AttemptFailedTransition
	KILL	**KILLED**	KillAppAndAttemptTransition
REMOVING	NODE_UPDATE	**REMOVING**	
	KILL	**KILLED**	KillAppAndAttemptTransition
	APP_REMOVED	**FINISHING**	RMAppFinishingTransition
	ATTEMPT_FINISHED	**FINISHED**	FINISHED_TRANSITION

Current State	Event Occurred	New State	Event Class Instantiated
FINISHING	NODE_UPDATE, APP_REMOVED	FINISHING	
	ATTEMPT_FINISHED	FINISHED	FINISHED_TRANSITION
	KILL	FINISHED	KillAppAndAttemptTransition
FINISHED	NODE_UPDATE, ATTEMPT_ UNREGISTERED, ATTEMPT_FINISHED, KILL, APP_REMOVED	FINISHED	final state
FAILED	KILL, NODE_ UPDATE, APP_ SAVED, APP_ REMOVED	FAILED	final state
KILLED	APP_ACCEPTED, APP_REJECTED, KILL, ATTEMPT_ FINISHED, ATTEMPT_FAILED, ATTEMPT_KILLED, NODE_UPDATE, APP_SAVED, APP_ REMOVED	KILLED	final state

View 3 – An application attempt

ResourceManager's view of an application attempt represents the life cycle of each attempt made by an application for its execution over the YARN cluster. As we have seen in the application life cycle, when an application is moved from **ACCEPTED** to **RUNNING**, an attempt of the application is registered with the ResourceManager. This section will cover the state management for an application attempt.

Here is the list of enumerations and classes involved:

- `org.apache.hadoop.yarn.server.resourcemanager.rmapp.attempt.RMAppAttempt`: This is an interface to an application attempt for the ResourceManager. An application can have multiple attempts based on maximum number of attempts configured.
- `org.apache.hadoop.yarn.server.resourcemanager.rmapp.attempt.RMAppAttemptImpl`: This class defines application attempt state transitions and access to the application's current attempt.
- `org.apache.hadoop.yarn.server.resourcemanager.rmapp.attempt.RMAppAttemptEventType`: This is an enumeration defining the different event types for an application attempt.
- `org.apache.hadoop.yarn.server.resourcemanager.rmapp.attempt.RMAppAttemptState`: This is an enumeration defining the different states of an application attempt.

The following state transition diagram explains the ResourceManager's view of an application attempt:

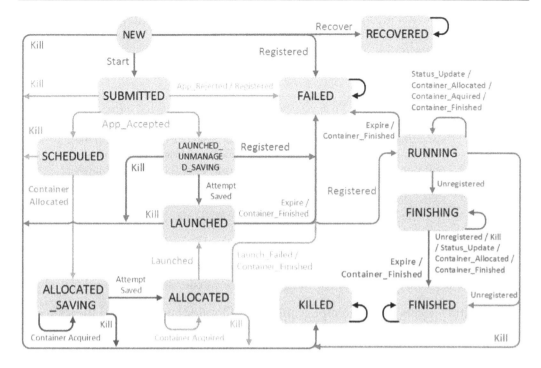

The start and final states of the ResourceManager's view of an application attempt container are as follows:

- Start state: **NEW**
- Final states: **FINISHED / EXPIRED / RELEASED / KILLED**

As the ResourceManager accepts an application successfully, an application attempt is initialized with the **NEW** state. A new `attemptId` is generated for the attempt and the attempt is added to the application's attempt list.

An `RMAppStartAttemptEvent` handler is invoked and the state of the attempt is changed to **SUBMITTED**. During the start attempt event, the attempt is first registered with `ApplicationMasterService` of ResourceManager. If the application is running in a secured mode, then the user is authenticated with the `client-token-master-key` in application, and the same key is available in the ResourceManager context. For more information about security in YARN, you can refer to *Chapter 11, Enabling Security in YARN Cluster*. An `AMRMToken` is generated and the attempt is added to scheduler.

The scheduler accepts the application attempt and allocates a container for the ApplicationMaster process, as per the requirements in the `ContainerLaunchContext` object. If the application is configured as an unmanaged AM, the attempt will be saved and the state is directly changed to **LAUNCHED**.

 Unmanaged AM: An application is said to be unmanaged if the ResourceManager does not manage the execution of ApplicationMaster. An unmanaged AM does not require allocation of a container and the ResourceManager will not start the ApplicationMaster service. The client will start the ApplicationMaster service only after the ResourceManager has `ACCEPTED` the application. If the ApplicationMaster fails to connect to the ResourceManager within the ApplicationMaster liveliness period, then the ResourceManager will mark the application as failed.

If the ApplicationMaster is to be executed in a managed environment, then the state of the attempt will be changed to **SCHEDULED**. The attempt then requests the scheduler to allocate a container for the ApplicationMaster service.

On successful allocation, the attempt acquires the allocated container and the state of attempt is changed to **ALLOCATED**. Once containers are allocated, ResourceManager will execute the command to start ApplicationMaster and the state of attempt is updated to **LAUNCHED**. ResourceManager waits for ApplicationMaster to register itself within the ApplicationMaster liveliness period, otherwise ResourceManager will mark the attempt as **FAILED**. ApplicationMaster registers itself with the host and port on which it is running and a tracking URL to monitor the progress of the application. ApplicationMaster also registers a communication client token with ResourceManager (`AMRMClient`) and NodeManager (`AMNMClient`).

ApplicationMaster will request for containers and manage the application execution. Once the attempt is finished, it is unregistered and moved to **FINISHING**, where the final state is stored and then the attempt is marked as **FINISHED**. At any state of attempt execution, if an exception occurs, the attempt is marked as **FAILED**. For example, if there's an error during the registration of an attempt, then the attempt is rejected. Similarly, when we manage ApplicationMaster and there are insufficient resources to launch the ApplicationMaster, the launch event fails and the attempt is marked as **FAILED**.

If a client sends a signal to kill an application, then its attempt or all associated containers are directly marked as **KILLED**. A `KillAllocatedAMTransition` handle is invoked and cleanup tasks are executed.

Here is a summarized table view for ResourceManager's view of an application attempt:

Current State	Event Occurred	New State	Event Class Instantiated
NEW	START	SUBMITTED	`AttemptStartedTransition`
	KILL	KILLED	`BaseFinalTransition`
	REGISTERED	FAILED	`UnexpectedAMRegistered Transition`
	RECOVER	RECOVERED	
SUBMITTED	APP_REJECTED	FAILED	`AppRejectedTransition`
	APP_ACCEPTED	LAUNCHED_ UNMANAGED_ SAVING / SCHEDULED	`ScheduleTransition`
	KILL	KILLED	`BaseFinalTransition`
	REGISTERED	FAILED	`UnexpectedAMRegistered Transition`
SCHEDULED	CONTAINER_ ALLOCATED	ALLOCATED_ SAVING	`AMContainerAllocated Transition`
	KILL	KILLED	`BaseFinalTransition`
ALLOCATED_ SAVING	ATTEMPT_SAVED	ALLOCATED	`AttemptStoredTransition`
	CONTAINER_ ACQUIRED	ALLOCATED_ SAVING	`ContainerAcquiredTransition`
	KILL	KILLED	`BaseFinalTransition`
LAUNCHED_ UNMANAGED_ SAVING	ATTEMPT_SAVED	LAUNCHED	`UnmanagedAMAttemptSaved Transition`
	REGISTERED	FAILED	`UnexpectedAMRegistered Transition`
	KILL	KILLED	`BaseFinalTransition`
ALLOCATED	CONTAINER_ ACQUIRED	ALLOCATED	`ContainerAcquiredTransition`
	LAUNCHED	LAUNCHED	`AMLaunchedTransition`
	LAUNCH_FAILED	FAILED	`LaunchFailedTransition`
	KILL	KILLED	`KillAllocatedAMTransition`
	CONTAINER_ FINISHED	FAILED	`AMContainerCrashedTransition`
LAUNCHED	REGISTERED	RUNNING	`AMRegisteredTransition`
	CONTAINER_ FINISHED	FAILED	`AMContainerCrashedTransition`
	EXPIRE	FAILED	`EXPIRED_TRANSITION`
	KILL	KILLED	`FinalTransition`

Current State	Event Occurred	New State	Event Class Instantiated
RUNNING	UNREGISTERED	**FINISHING/ FINISHED**	`AMUnregisteredTransition`
	STATUS_UPDATE	**RUNNING**	`StatusUpdateTransition`
	CONTAINER_ ALLOCATED	**RUNNING**	
	CONTAINER_ ACQUIRED	**RUNNING**	`ContainerAcquiredTransition`
	CONTAINER_ FINISHED	**RUNNING/ FAILED**	`ContainerFinishedTransition`
	EXPIRE	**FAILED**	`EXPIRED_TRANSITION`
	KILL	**KILLED**	`FinalTransition`
FINISHING	CONTAINER_ FINISHED	**FINISHING/ FINISHED**	`AMFinishingContainerFinished Transition`
	EXPIRE	**FINISHED**	`FinalTransition`
	UNREGISTERED / STATUS_UPDATE /CONTAINER_ ALLOCATED/KILL	**FINISHING**	
FAILED	EXPIRE / KILL / UNREGISTERED / STATUS_UPDATE /CONTAINER_ ALLOCATED/ CONTAINER_ FINISHED	**FAILED**	final state
FINISHED	EXPIRE / KILL / UNREGISTERED / CONTAINER_ ALLOCATED/ CONTAINER_ FINISHED	**FINISHED**	final state
KILLED	APP_ACCEPTED / APP_REJECTED / EXPIRE / LAUNCHED / LAUNCH_FAILED /EXPIRE / REGISTERED / STATUS_UPDATE / CONTAINER_ ALLOCATED/ ATTEMPT_SAVED /CONTAINER_ FINISHED / UNREGISTERED / KILL	**KILLED**	final state

Current State	Event Occurred	New State	Event Class Instantiated
RECOVERED	START / APP_ ACCEPTED / APP_REJECTED / EXPIRE / LAUNCHED / LAUNCH_FAILED /EXPIRE / REGISTERED / STATUS_UPDATE / CONTAINER_ ALLOCATED/ ATTEMPT_SAVED /CONTAINER_ FINISHED / UNREGISTERED / KILL	**RECOVERED**	final state

View 4 – Container

ResourceManager manages the life cycle of all the requested containers. An application demands the container application execution and releases containers back to ResourceManager after the application is finished. The ResourceManager stores the metadata related to each container and schedules the applications accordingly.

The metadata of a container includes:

- **Container ID**: This is a unique ID for all the containers
- **Application attempt ID**: This is the application attempt ID associated with the container
- **Node ID**: This is the reserved and allocated node for the container
- **Resource**: This is the memory and virtual cores
- **Time-Stamps**: This is the creation and finish time
- **States**: This includes `ContainerState` and `RMContainerState`
- **Monitoring info**: This is the container's diagnostic information and logs URL

Here is the list of enumerations and classes involved:

- `org.apache.hadoop.yarn.server.resourcemanager.rmcontainer. RMContainer`: This is an interface to a container for the ResourceManager. It stores container properties such as its priority, creation time, attempt ID, and so on.
- `org.apache.hadoop.yarn.server.resourcemanager.rmcontainer. RMContainerImpl`: This class defines container state transitions and associated event handlers.

- org.apache.hadoop.yarn.server.resourcemanager.rmcontainer. RMContainerEventType: This is an enumeration defining the different event type for a container.
- org.apache.hadoop.yarn.server.resourcemanager.rmcontainer. RMContainerState: This is an enumeration defining the different states of a container.

The following state transition diagram explains the ResourceManager's view of a container:

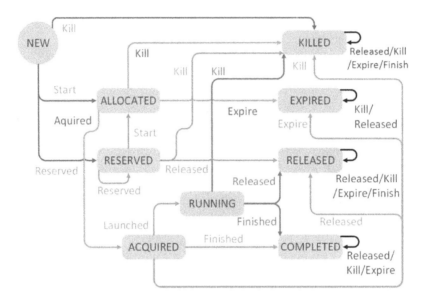

The start and final states of the ResourceManager's view of a container are as follows:

- Start state: **NEW**
- Final states: **COMPLETED** / **EXPIRED** / **RELEASED** / **KILLED**

ResourceManager instantiates a new instance of RMContainer as the request for containers is accepted. The container is either allocated to the application or an application attempt can reserve a container when the container is in the **NEW** state by calling up the Reserved event.

ApplicationMaster acquires the allocated containers and the state of the container is updated to **ACQUIRED**. The container creation time and allocated node information is saved with container context. ApplicationMaster communicates with NodeManager and executes the command to start the container. The container is launched on the allocated node and the state is changed to **RUNNING**.

After successful execution, the finished event is called and the container is marked as **COMPLETED**. ApplicationMaster releases the memory occupied by the completed containers back to ResourceManager, and the `FinishedTransition` handle is invoked. The finish time, finished status, exit status, and diagnostic information is captured. If a container in the **RUNNING** state is directly released, the state of the container is changed to **RELEASED** and the `KillTransition` handle is invoked.

At any state of execution, the container is being monitored for liveliness and expiration. If the expiration time is reached at any state, the execution of the container is stopped and the container is marked as **EXPIRED**. Similarly, at any state, if a container receives a kill signal, it directly moves up to the **KILLED** state.

Here is a summarized table view for ResourceManager's view of a container:

Current State	Event Occurred	New State	Event Class Instantiated
NEW	START	ALLOCATED	ContainerStarted Transition
	RESERVED	RESERVED	ContainerReserved Transition
	KILL	KILLED	
RESERVED	START	ALLOCATED	ContainerStarted Transition
	RESERVED	RESERVED	ContainerReserved Transition
	KILL	KILLED	
	RELEASED	RELEASED	
ALLOCATED	ACQUIRED	ACQUIRED	AcquiredTransition
	EXPIRE	EXPIRED	FinishedTransition
	KILL	KILLED	FinishedTransition

Current State	Event Occurred	New State	Event Class Instantiated
ACQUIRED	LAUNCHED	RUNNING	LaunchedTransition
	FINISHED	COMPLETED	ContainerFinishedAt AcquiredState
	RELEASED	RELEASED	KillTransition
	EXPIRE	EXPIRED	KillTransition
	KILL	KILLED	KillTransition
RUNNING	FINISHED	COMPLETED	FinishedTransition
	RELEASED	RELEASED	KillTransition
	EXPIRE	RUNNING	
	KILL	KILLED	KillTransition
COMPLETED	KILL, RELEASED, EXPIRE	COMPLETED	final state
EXPIRED	KILL, RELEASED	EXPIRED	final state
RELEASED	KILL, RELEASED, EXPIRE, FINISHED	RELEASED	final state
KILLED	KILL, RELEASED, EXPIRE, FINISHED	KILLED	final state

This completes the ResourceManager's view for YARN processes. To read more about the transitions or events, you can refer to the implementation classes referred to in each section. In the next section, you'll learn about the NodeManager's view of YARN.

The NodeManager's view

The NodeManager service in YARN updates its resource capabilities to the ResourceManager and tracks the execution of containers running on the node.

Other than the health of a node, the NodeManager service is responsible for the following:

- Execution of an application and its associated containers
- Provide localized resources for the execution of containers related to applications
- Manage logs of different applications

The NodeManager service has its own view for the following:

- **Application**: This manages the application's execution, logs, and resources
- **Container**: This manages the execution of containers as a separate process
- **Localized resource**: This involves the files required for the container's execution

View 1 – Application

NodeManager manages the life cycle of the application's containers and resources used during application execution. The NodeManager view of an application represents how NodeManager manages the container's execution, resources, and logs of the application.

Here is the list of enumerations and classes involved. All these classes are defined under the `org.apache.hadoop.yarn.server.nodemanager.containermanager.application` package.

- `Application`: This is an interface to an application for the NodeManager. It stores application metadata only.
- `ApplicationImpl`: This class defines application state transitions and associated event handlers.
- `ApplicationEventType`: This is an enumeration that defines the different event types for an application.
- `ApplicationState`: This is an enumeration defining the different states for an application.

The NodeManager service stores only the basic information related to an application. The application metadata includes:

- The application ID
- The application state with respect to NodeManager
- The list of associated containers
- The user name

The following state transition diagram explains the NodeManager's view of an application:

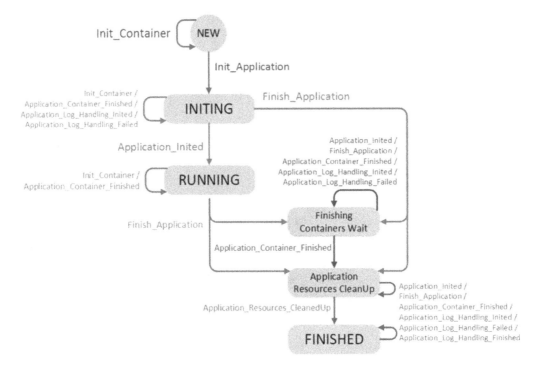

The start and final states of the NodeManager's view of an application are as follows:

- Start state: **NEW**
- Final states: **FINISHED**

During an application execution, the ApplicationMaster service runs as the first container for an application. ResourceManager accepts the application request and allocates resources for the ApplicationMaster service. The ContainerManager service within NodeManager accepts the application and starts the ApplicationMaster service on the node.

NodeManager marks the state of an application as **NEW**, initializes the application, and changes the application state to **INITING**. In this transition, the log aggregator service is initialized, along with the application's access control lists. If there's an exception while initializing the application or creating log directories, then the application remains in the **INITING** state and NodeManager sends warning messages to the user. NodeManager waits for either the `Application_Inited` or `Finish_Application` event.

> If log aggregation is enabled and the creation of log directory fails, a warning message such as `Log Aggregation service failed to initialize, there will be no logs for this application` is logged.

If `Application_Inited` gets completed, the state of the application is changed to **RUNNING**. The application requests and releases a number of containers during execution. Events such as `Application_Container_Finished` and `Container_Done_Transition` update the container list for the application and the state of the application is unchanged.

As the application finishes, the `Finish_Application` event is triggered. NodeManager waits for execution of all currently running containers for that application. The state of the application is changed to **Finishing Containers Wait**. After completion of all containers, the NodeManager service cleans up the resources used by the application and performs log aggregation for the application. Once the resources are cleaned up, the application is marked as **FINISHED**.

View 2 – Container

As discussed earlier, the NodeManager service is responsible for providing resources, containers execution, clean up, and so on. The life cycle of a container with NodeManager is defined in the `org.apache.hadoop.yarn.server.nodemanager.containermanager.container` package.

Here is the list of enumerations and classes involved:

- `Container`: This is an interface to a container for the NodeManager
- `ContainerImpl`: This class defines container state transitions and associated event handlers
- `ContainerEventType`: This is an enumeration defining the different event type for a container
- `ContainerState`: This is an enumeration defining the different states for a container

The following state transition diagram explains the NodeManager's view of a container:

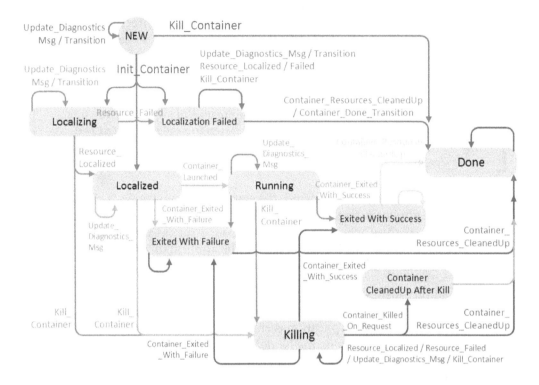

The start and final states of the NodeManager's view of a container are as follows:

- Start state: **NEW**
- Final states: **Done**

ResourceManager allocates containers on a particular node. As the containers are acquired by an application, the NodeManager initializes the container's object for the node. NodeManager requests the `ResourceLocalizationManager` service to download the resources required to run the container and marks the container state as **Localizing**.

For localization, the specified auxiliary service is informed. The auxiliary service has the information about the service data for the container. The `Resource_Localized` event is triggered when resources are successfully localized. If resources are already localized or resources are not required, then the container directly enters into the **Localized** state. If the resource localization fails, then the state of the container is changed to **Localization Failed**. The container launch is skipped if it directly moves to the **Done** state.

Once the container's resource requirements are met, the `Container_Launched` event is triggered and the container state is changed to **Running**. In this transition, the `ContainersMonitor` service is being informed to monitor the resource usage of the container. The NodeManager waits for the completion of the container. If the container is successfully executed, then a success event is invoked and the exit status of the container is marked as `0`. The container's state is changed to `EXITED_WITH_SUCCESS`. If the container fails, then the exit code and diagnostic information is updated and the state of the container is changed to `EXITED_WITH_FAILURE`.

At any stage, if a container receives a kill signal, the container is moved to the `KILLING` state, where the container cleanup is done and the state is later changed to `Container_CleanedUp_After_Kill`. It is mandatory for a container to clean up the resources used for its execution. When the resources are cleaned up, the `Container_Resources_CleanedUp` event is invoked and the state is marked as `DONE`.

View 3 – A localized resource

Resource localization is defined as downloading resource files before the execution of a container. For example, if a container requires a `jar` file for its execution, a localized resource is configured in `ContainerLaunchContext`. It is the responsibility of the NodeManager service to download the resource file on the local filesystem of the node. To find out more about resource localization, you can refer to *Chapter 8, Dive Deep into YARN Components*.

The NodeManager service maintains a life cycle for localized resources. NodeManager stores information related to a resource. The information includes:

- The resource path on the local filesystem
- The size of the resource
- The list of containers using the resource
- The resource visibility, type, pattern, and download path
- (`LocalResourceRequest`): The life cycle of a localized resource with NodeManager is defined in the `org.apache.hadoop.yarn.server.nodemanager.containermanager.localizer` package
- `LocalizedResource`: This class stores resource information, defines the state transitions and associated event handlers
- `ResourceState`: This is an enumeration defining the different states for a resource
- `event.ResourceEventType`: This is an enumeration defining the different event types for a resource

The following state transition diagram explains the NodeManager's view of a resource:

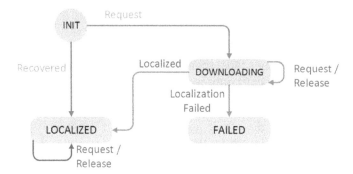

The start and final states of the NodeManager's view of a resource are as follows:

- Start state: **INIT**
- Final states: **LOCALIZED / FAILED**

As specified in the NodeManager's view of a container, resource localization is initiated during the INIT_CONTAINER event. The resources specified in the container launch context are initialized with INIT state.

When a resource is requested, a FetchResourceTransition handle is invoked and it initializes the resource details such as location, visibility, context, and so on. The state of the resource is changed to **DOWNLOADING**.

Once the resource is downloaded successfully, the resource state is marked as **LOCALIZED** and the resource path, size, and references are updated. If the localization of the resource fails, then the resource is marked as **FAILED** and the context is updated with a diagnostic message containing the reason of failure.

If there's any subsequent requests for a resource in the **DOWNLOADING** or **LOCALIZED** state, the handle to the path and context of the local resource is provided.

Multiple containers can use the same resource at the same time. The NodeManager service maintains a queue of containers for each localized resource. A container reference is added to the queue during a resource request, and is removed from the queue after resource release.

Analyzing transitions through logs

Both YARN services, ResourceManager and NodeManager generate logs and store them in a `.log` file locally inside the folder specified using the `HADOOP_LOGS_DIR` variable. By default, the logs are stored in `HADOOP_PREFIX/logs`. All the state transitions in YARN are recorded in the log files. In this section, we'll cover few state transitions and the logs generated during those transitions.

> **Setting the log level**: Hadoop-YARN uses Apache `Log4j` library and it uses a `log4j.properties` file located in the configuration folder of the Hadoop-YARN bundle at `HADOOP_PREFIX/etc/hadoop`.
>
> The `Log4j` library supports six log levels – `TRACE`, `DEBUG`, `INFO`, `WARN`, `ERROR`, and `FATAL`. A cluster administrator sets the log level for Hadoop-YARN services and the default log level is `INFO`. The `hadoop.root.logger` property is used to update the log level for Hadoop-YARN services. To read more about Apache `Log4j` library, you can refer to the official site at `http://logging.apache.org/log4j/`.

NodeManager registration with ResourceManager

The ResourceManager consists of ResourceTracker service that is responsible for monitoring of the resources across the cluster. A NodeManager service registers itself to the ResourceManager service. The registration information contains the ports used and the memory information of the node. After successful registration, the state of the node is changed from **NEW** to **RUNNING**.

You can refer to the following ResourceManager's logs during NodeManager registration:

```
2014-10-25 08:24:15,183 INFO
org.apache.hadoop.yarn.server.resourcemanager.ResourceTrackerService:
NodeManager from node master(cmPort: 37594 httpPort: 8042) registered
with capability: <memory:8192, vCores:8>, assigned nodeId
master:37594

2014-10-25 08:24:28,079 INFO
org.apache.hadoop.yarn.server.resourcemanager.rmnode.RMNodeImpl:
master:37594 Node Transitioned from NEW to RUNNING
```

Application submission

The following ResourceManager logs describe the state transitions during application execution. The `ClientRMService` state assigns a new application ID and `RMAppImpl` initializes the application object with the NEW state. Once the application is submitted, a queue is assigned and the state of the application changes from SUBMITTED to ACCEPTED.

```
org.apache.hadoop.yarn.server.resourcemanager.ClientRMService:
Allocated new applicationId: 1
```

```
org.apache.hadoop.yarn.server.resourcemanager.rmapp.RMAppImpl:
Storing application with id application_1414205634577_0001
```

```
org.apache.hadoop.yarn.server.resourcemanager.rmapp.RMAppImpl:
application_1414205634577_0001 State change from NEW to NEW_SAVING
```

```
org.apache.hadoop.yarn.server.resourcemanager.recovery.RMStateStore:
Storing info for app: application_1414205634577_0001
```

```
org.apache.hadoop.yarn.server.resourcemanager.rmapp.RMAppImpl:
application_1414205634577_0001 State change from NEW_SAVING to
SUBMITTED
```

```
org.apache.hadoop.yarn.server.resourcemanager.scheduler.capacity.Pare
ntQueue: Application added - appId: application_1414205634577_0001
user: akhil leaf-queue of parent: root #applications: 1
```

```
org.apache.hadoop.yarn.server.resourcemanager.scheduler.capacity.Capa
cityScheduler: Accepted application application_1414205634577_0001
from user: akhil, in queue: default
```

```
org.apache.hadoop.yarn.server.resourcemanager.rmapp.RMAppImpl:
application_1414205634577_0001 State change from SUBMITTED to
ACCEPTED
```

Container resource allocation

The ResourceManager scheduler is responsible for allocating containers to YARN applications. The following logs describe the details of the assigned container (container ID, memory, and cores assigned). It also contains the summary of the assigned host, including the number of containers, memory used, and available memory after allocation.

```
org.apache.hadoop.yarn.server.resourcemanager.scheduler.SchedulerNode
: Assigned container container_1414205634577_0001_01_000003 of
capacity <memory:1024, vCores:1> on host master:37594, which has 3
containers, <memory:4096, vCores:3> used and <memory:4096, vCores:5>
available after allocation
```

Resource localization

The NodeManager service is responsible for providing resources required during execution of containers. The resources are downloaded from the supported source (such as HDFS, HTTP, and so on) to the NodeManager node's local directory.

You can refer to the following NodeManager log during resource localization:

```
2014-10-25 14:01:26,224 INFO
org.apache.hadoop.yarn.server.nodemanager.containermanager.localizer.
LocalizedResource: Resource hdfs://master:8020/tmp/hadoop-
yarn/staging/akhil/.staging/job_1414205634577_0001/job.splitmetainfo(
->/tmp/hadoop-akhil/nm-local-
dir/usercache/akhil/appcache/application_1414205634577_0001/filecache
/10/job.splitmetainfo) transitioned from DOWNLOADING to LOCALIZED
```

Summary

In this chapter, we learned about the state management analogy of YARN and why it is important. We discussed about the ResourceManager and NodeManager views for the different processes associated with the YARN framework. This chapter provides core concepts about how YARN monitors and manages the resources or application execution over YARN. You can now easily scan the logs for ResourceManager or NodeManager and observe the messages during state transitions of a node, an application, or a container, and so on.

In the next chapter, we'll talk about the execution of MapReduce applications over a YARN cluster and how you can migrate from MRv1 to MRv2.

6
Migrating from MRv1 to MRv2

Hadoop development started in 2005 and in December 2011, it reached version 1.0.0. Enterprises started using Hadoop and implemented data processing algorithms based on the MapReduce programming framework. In 2013, Hadoop version 2.2.0 was released and the MapReduce framework went through a lot of architectural changes. A generic framework for resource management, that is, YARN was introduced and architecture for MapReduce job execution over a Hadoop cluster changed. The old API of the framework is known as MRv1 and the MapReduce APIs associated with YARN framework are termed as MRv2.

In this chapter, we will cover the following:

- Introduction MRv1 and MRv2
- Migrating to MRv2
- Running and monitoring MRv1 apps on YARN

Introducing MRv1 and MRv2

The MapReduce framework in Hadoop 1.x version is also known as MRv1. The MRv1 framework includes client communication, job execution and management, resource scheduling and resource management. The Hadoop daemons associated with MRv1 are **JobTracker** and **TaskTracker** as shown in the following figure:

JobTracker	Scheduling
	Resource Management
	Job Management
TaskTracker	Job Execution

JobTracker is a master service responsible for client communications, MapReduce job management, scheduling, resource management, and so on. The **TaskTracker** service is a worker daemon that runs on every slave of the Hadoop cluster. It is responsible for the execution of map reduce tasks. A client submits a job to the **JobTracker** service. The **JobTracker** validates the request and breaks the job into tasks. The **JobTracker** uses a data localization mechanism and assigns **TaskTracker** for the execution of tasks. The **TaskTracker** service runs a map reduce task as a separate JVM named as child as described in the following figure:

Resource Manager	Scheduling
	Resource Management
Application Master	Job Management
Node Manager	Job Execution

The following diagram shows the MRv1 services and their equivalent MRv2 services:

JobTracker and **TaskTracker** services in YARN are no longer used. The MRv2 framework uses **ResourceManager** and **MRApplicationMaster** services instead of the JobTracker service. Also, the **NodeManager** service replaces the **TaskTracker** service.

High-level changes from MRv1 to MRv2

With the introduction of YARN, the architecture for Hadoop job execution and management framework changed. In this section, we'll discuss the list of high-level changes observed in MRv2 framework.

The evolution of the MRApplicationMaster service

In YARN, the responsibility of JobTracker is divided across the ResourceManager service and application-specific ApplicationMaster service. For management of MapReduce jobs, MRApplicationMaster service is defined in the Hadoop framework. For each MapReduce job submitted to ResourceManager, an instance MRApplicationMaster service is launched. After successful execution of the job, the MRApplicationMaster service is terminated.

The MRApplicationMaster service is responsible for:

- Registering the job with the ResourceManager
- Negotiating YARN containers for execution of map reduce tasks
- Interacting with NodeManager to manage execution of allocated containers
- Handling task failure and reinitiate failed tasks
- Handling client request for job status through REST API / Web UI

The implementation of MRApplicationMaster is defined in the `org.apache.hadoop.mapreduce.v2.app` package. For more information about the `MRAppMaster` class, you can refer to the Java class at:

`http://www.grepcode.com/file/repo1.maven.org/maven2/org.apache.hadoop/hadoop-mapreduce-client-app/2.5.1/org/apache/hadoop/mapreduce/v2/app/MRAppMaster.java`.

Resource capability

In MRv1, the capability of a slave node is measured as the maximum number of map reduce task slots available for task execution. In MRv2, the resource capability of a node is measured in terms of the memory and virtual cores that are available for task execution. The properties for defining the maximum map reduce tasks associated with a node are no longer used. A detailed description about these properties is given in the next section.

Pluggable shuffle

During MapReduce job execution, the output of the map function is copied to the node selected for reduce task. This phase during a MapReduce job is known as shuffling. The YARN framework allows users to define a shuffle mechanism that can be used for data transfer during job execution. The configuration for shuffle mechanism is discussed in the next section.

Hierarchical queues and fair scheduler

YARN schedulers support for hierarchical queues. Queues have a parent-child relationship and the fair scheduler uses queues instead of pools. The properties for the fair scheduler, such as `minMaps`, `minReduces`, `maxMaps`, and so on, are now deprecated and are replaced by `minResources`, `maxResources`, and so on. To read more about the schedulers, you can refer to *Chapter 10, Scheduling YARN Applications*.

Task execution as containers

A container is a simple notation for a block of memory and virtual cores used by a task. In MRv2, the map reduce tasks run as a YARN container known as `YARNChild`. For more information, you can also refer to the implementation of a `YARNChild` class at `http://grepcode.com/file/repo1.maven.org/maven2/org.apache.hadoop/hadoop-mapreduce-client-app/2.5.1/org/apache/hadoop/mapred/YarnChild.java`.

The migration steps from MRv1 to MRv2

The migration steps from MRv1 to MRv2 can be categorized as:

- The configuration changes to use YARN as the MapReduce execution framework
- The binary / source compatibility while working with MapReduce APIs

Configuration changes

In this section, we'll discuss the configuration changes required during migration from MRv1 to MRv2. The information provided in this section is limited to the minimum configuration changes required during the migration. Detailed information regarding the deprecated and new properties is provided in a Cloudera blog at `https://www.cloudera.com/content/cloudera/en/documentation/core/v5-2-x/topics/cdh_ig_mapreduce_to_yarn_migrate.html`.

The upcoming sections describe the changes while migrating from MRv1 to MRv2.

- The MapReduce framework

  If you recall the configuration of a Hadoop cluster in MRv1, the `mapred-site.xml` file contains the host information related to the JobTracker service. In MRv2, the following property in the `mapred-site.xml` file contains the configuration for the MapReduce framework to be used:

  ```
  <property>
      <name>mapreduce.framework.name</name>
      <value>yarn</value>
  </property>
  ```

  A cluster administrator can define any of the three MapReduce frameworks (`local` / `classic` / `yarn`). To enable YARN, the value of the property should be set to `yarn`. To find out more about the `local` and `classic` mode, you can refer to *Chapter 2*, *Setting up a Hadoop-YARN Cluster*.

- The ResourceManager host

  In the MapReduce framework specified in `mapred-site.xml` is yarn, then you need to define host for ResourceManager service. A cluster administrator needs to configure the following property containing the hostname or IP for the ResourceManager node:

  ```
  <property>
      <name>yarn.resourcemanager.hostname</name>
      <value>master</value>
  </property>
  ```

Properties such as `yarn.resourcemanager.address`, `yarn.resourcemanager.webapp.address`, `yarn.resourcemanager.admin.address`, and so on will automatically reuse the value of the ResourceManager host specified in the property we just saw and will use the default port settings. If you wish to change the default ports, you can define these properties in the `yarn-site.xml` file in the `host:port` format.

To read more about default ResourceManager properties, you can refer to the `yarn-default.xml` at `http://hadoop.apache.org/docs/r2.5.1/hadoop-yarn/hadoop-yarn-common/yarn-default.xml`.

- The shuffle service

  As mentioned in the previous section, the shuffle service in the MapReduce job moves the map task's output to reduce the task nodes. YARN provides an option to configure AUX services used during application execution. An administrator needs to define the MapReduce shuffle service as an AUX service for the YARN cluster. It can be configured using the following properties in the `yarn-site.xml` file:

```
<property>
    <name>yarn.nodemanager.aux-services</name>
    <value>mapreduce_shuffle</value>
</property>

<property>
    <name>yarn.nodemanager.aux-
services.mapreduce_shuffle.class</name>
    <value>org.apache.hadoop.mapred.ShuffleHandler</value>
</property>
```

- The scheduler configuration

  The default scheduler in MRv1 is **First In First Out (FIFO)**, but in MRv2 the default scheduler is `CapacityScheduler`. A cluster administrator needs to specify the class for scheduling using the following property:

```
<property>
<name>yarn.resourcemanager.scheduler.class</name>
<value>org.apache.hadoop.yarn.server.resourcemanager.scheduler.cap
acity.CapacityScheduler</value>
</property>
```

- The resource capability

  As mentioned in the previous section, the resource capability of a node in YARN is calculated as the memory and virtual cores available for container execution. The MRv1 properties `mapred.tasktracker.map.tasks.maximum`, `mapred.tasktracker.reduce.tasks.maximum`, and so on for defining the `mapreduce` tasks associated with a node are no longer used. An administrator can use the following properties in the `mapred-site.xml` file to define the memory each `mapreduce` task can request from the scheduler:

  ```
  <property>
      <name>mapreduce.map.memory.mb</name>
      <value>1536</value>
  </property>

  <property>
      <name>mapreduce.reduce.memory.mb</name>
      <value>2560</value>
  </property>
  ```

  In MRv1, the `mapred.child.java.opts` property in the `mapred-site.xml` file is used to define the hard limits on each map reduce task. In MRv2, the hard limit of tasks is defined using the following properties in the `mapred-site.xml` file:

  ```
  <property>
      <name>mapreduce.map.java.opts</name>
      <value>-Xmx1024m</value>
  </property>

  <property>
      <name>mapreduce.reduce.java.opts</name>
      <value>-Xmx2048m</value>
  </property>
  ```

  To understand the recommended memory configuration settings, you can refer to an HDP blog at `http://docs.hortonworks.com/HDPDocuments/HDP2/HDP-2.1.2/bk_installing_manually_book/content/rpm-chap1-11.html`.

The binary / source compatibility

One of the major concerns while migrating is the compatibility of MapReduce's existing source and binary files written using MRv1 classes. If an enterprise adopts YARN, then will the programs developed with old APIs work with the new framework? The answer is yes for binary files, but it is not 100 percent true for source code.

If a developer needs to execute an MRv1 job using a binary file (executable `jar` file) on a Hadoop-YARN, then the job execution will be similar to execution in MRv1. All the binaries will work on the new framework. To verify this, you can use any of the old `hadoop-examples-<version 1.x>.jar` command and execute the `yarn` application submission command:

```
yarn jar <jarPath><class><args>
```

If a developer needs to execute a MapReduce job using source code, then the developer first needs to compile and build the source code against the new Hadoop-YARN libraries. Most of the MRv1 classes exist in the new framework, but there are some minor changes in the API.

A summary of the API changes is available at `http://docs.hortonworks.com/HDPDocuments/HDP2/HDP-2.1.2/bk_using-apache-hadoop/content/running_hadoop_v1_apps_on_yarn.html`.

Running and monitoring MRv1 apps on YARN

The syntax to submit applications is similar to the MRv1 framework. A minor difference in MRv2 is the use of the `yarn` command in the Hadoop-YARN `bin` folder rather than hadoop. Although submission of applications is supported using the `hadoop` command in MRv2, the `yarn` command is still preferred.

YARN uses the ResourceManager web interface for monitoring applications running on a YARN cluster. The ResourceManager UI shows the basic cluster metrics, list of applications, and nodes associated with the cluster. In this section, we'll discuss the monitoring of MRv1 applications over YARN.

You can execute a sample MapReduce job like word count and browse to the web UI for ResourceManager at `http://<ResourceManagerHost>:8088/`.

A new application is submitted to the YARN cluster and you can view the application summary in the application table. You can open the application details page by clicking on the link for the corresponding row in the table.

The application details page is the same for all applications in YARN. It contains the information related to the application's state, attempts, and so on, as shown in the following figure:

You can observe that if the application is in the **RUNNING** state, then the **Tracking URL** on the application details page refers to the **ApplicationMaster** page. On clicking the link for **ApplicationMaster**, you will be redirected to the web UI of **MRApplicationMaster**. This page contains running the status of a job including the job ID, the number of map reduce tasks, the current state, and so on.

To view the job status in detail, you can click on the link with the **Job ID**. A new page will open and it'll contain a detailed view of job statistics. You can also browse through several links in the **Jobs** menu on the left side of the page such as overview, counters, configuration, tasks, and so on. You can refer to any of the links to get the required information.

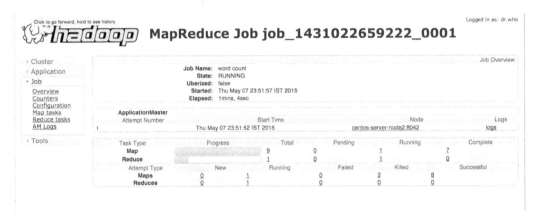

The web-UI for MRApplicationMaster is available only until the application is in running state. Once the application is finished, the MRApplicationMaster web UI is not available. You will see that the tracking URL on the application details page changes to **History**.

There are two different terminologies for application state for an application in YARN—State and FinalStatus. The **FinalStatus** of an application represents the final state of the MapReduce job and the **State** represents the overall state of the YARN application. You can refer to the following screenshot, which shows that the state of the application is **FINISHED**, but the **FinalStatus** of the MapReduce job is **FAILED**, as given in the following screenshot:

Summary

With the adoption of YARN with Hadoop, the architecture for MapReduce programming framework and APIs were modified and the new framework is named MRv2. This chapter covered a brief about the differences between MRv1 and MRv2. It also explained the configuration changes, code compatibility, and monitoring of MRv1 applications when administrators and developers migrate from MRv1 to MRv2.

In the next chapter, you'll learn about writing your own YARN applications. This requires you to have basic knowledge of Java programming and is focused for developers who are eager to learn application development that is compatible with YARN.

Writing Your Own YARN Applications

7

In the first chapter, we talked about the shortcomings of Hadoop 1.x framework. Hadoop 1.x framework was restricted to MapReduce programming only. You had to write data processing logic as map and reduce tasks. With the introduction of YARN in Hadoop 2.x version, you can now execute different data processing algorithms over the data stored in HDFS. YARN separates the resource management and the data processing frameworks into two different components, ResourceManager and ApplicationMaster.

In the last few chapters, you learned about the application execution flow, and how YARN components communicate and manage the life cycle of an application. You executed a MapReduce application over a YARN cluster and worked with `MRApplicationMaster` component. In this chapter, you will learn to create your own YARN applications using YARN Java APIs. This chapter requires you to have a Java background and basic knowledge of Eclipse IDE. This chapter is helpful for developers and open source contributors who want to create and execute applications over a YARN cluster.

In this chapter, we will cover the following topics:

- Introduction to the YARN API
- Key concepts and classes involved
- Writing your own application
- Executing applications over the Hadoop-YARN cluster

An introduction to the YARN API

YARN is a Java framework that is packaged with the Hadoop bundle. YARN provides resource management, as well as easy integration of data processing or accessing algorithms for data stored in Hadoop HDFS. Apache Storm, Giraph, and HAMA are few examples of the data processing algorithms that use YARN for resource management. A detailed integration of such technologies is covered in *Chapter 12, Real-time Data Analytics Using YARN*.

The Hadoop-YARN API is defined in the `org.apache.hadoop.yarn.api` package. While writing your own YARN applications, you will use some of the classes from the YARN API. Before moving ahead, it is important to list the classes used and understand their role. This section will cover a few important classes defined in the `org.apache.hadoop.yarn.api` package.

YARNConfiguration

The `YARNConfiguration` class is defined in the `org.apache.hadoop.yarn.conf` package and it extends the `org.apache.hadoop.conf.Configuration` class. Similar to the `Configuration` class, it reads the YARN configuration files (`yarn-default.xml` and `yarn-site.xml`) and provides access to Hadoop-YARN configuration parameters. The following are the responsibilities of the `YARNConfiguration` class:

Load resources

The Hadoop configuration files contain name / value properties as XML data. The files are loaded in the order they are added. The `YARNConfiguration` class will load the `yarn-default.xml` file and then the `yarn-site.xml` file. The value specified in the `yarn-site.xml` file will be used. The properties specified in `*-site.xml` are overridden over those in `*-default.xml` and rest are referred from `*-default.xml`.

Consider the following example, where a property has a default value in `yarn-default.xml` and a user defines the same property in `yarn-site.xml`. The following property is defined in the `yarn-default.xml` file:

```
<property>
<name>yarn.resourcemanager.hostname</name>
<value>0.0.0.0</value>
</property>
```

And you have specified the same property in `yarn-site.xml` as follows:

```
<property>
<name>yarn.resourcemanager.hostname</name>
<value>masternode</value>
</property>
```

The `YARNConfiguration` class will return the `masternode` value for `yarn.resourcemanager.hostname` property.

Final properties

A property may be declared as a `final` property. If an administrator does not want any client to update the `value` of any parameter, then the administrator will define the property as `final` as given in the following:

```
<property>
<name>yarn.acl.enable</name>
<value>true</value>
<final>true</final>
</property>
```

Variable expansion

The value for a property may contain variables as other properties defined in the configuration files or properties of the Java process. You can consider the following example for the `resourcemanager` hostname:

```
<property>
<name>yarn.resourcemanager.hostname</name>
<value>masternode</value>
</property>

<property>
<name>yarn.resourcemanager.webapp.address</name>
<value>${yarn.resourcemanager.hostname}:8088</value>
</property>
```

The value for the `yarn.resourcemanager.webapp.address` property is evaluated using the variable from the previous property.

 A commonly used Java system property used in YARN for variable expansion is `${user.name}`.

To read more about the YARNConfiguration class, you can refer to the Hadoop API documentation at http://hadoop.apache.org/docs/r2.5.1/api/org/apache/hadoop/yarn/conf/YarnConfiguration.html.

ApplicationSubmissionContext

ApplicationSubmissionContext is an abstract class containing the information to launch the ApplicationMaster for an application. The client defines the submission context containing the attributes of the application, command to run the ApplicationMaster service and list of resources required, and so on. During the application submission request, the client sends this context to the ResourceManager. The ResourceManager uses this context to save the application state and launch the ApplicationMaster process on a NodeManager node.

The ApplicationSubmissionContext class contains the following:

- The application ID, name, and type
- Queue and its priority
- AM container specification (ContainerLaunchContext for AM)
- Boolean flags for unmanaged AM and container management
- Number of maximum application attempts and resources required

To read more about the ApplicationSubmissionContext class, you can refer to the Hadoop API documentation at http://hadoop.apache.org/docs/r2.5.1/api/org/apache/hadoop/yarn/api/records/ApplicationSubmissionContext.html.

ContainerLaunchContext

ContainerLaunchContext is an abstract class containing information to start a container on a node. A NodeManager daemon uses the launch context to start containers associated with an application. An ApplicationMaster is the first container of an application and its launch context is defined in the ApplicationSubmissionContext class.

The ContainerLaunchContext objects contain the following:

- A map of the local resources used during startup
- A map for environment variables defined
- A list of commands used to start the container
- Information related to associated auxiliary services and tokens
- Application ACLs (application access type to view or modify the application)

To read more about the `ContainerLaunchContext` class, you can refer to the Hadoop API documentation at `http://hadoop.apache.org/docs/r2.5.1/api/org/apache/hadoop/yarn/api/records/ContainerLaunchContext.html`.

Communication protocols

The YARN API contains four communication protocols for interaction of YARN client and ApplicationMaster with YARN services such as ResourceManager, NodeManager, and Timeline server. These are defined in the `org.apache.hadoop.yarn.api` package. This section gives a brief description of these interfaces and their usage:

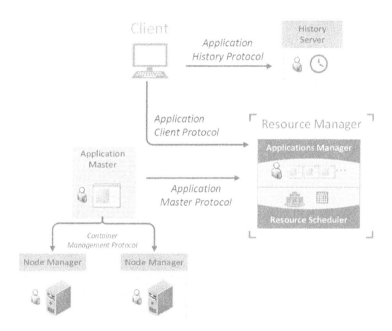

ApplicationClientProtocol

The `ApplicationClientProtocol` interface defines the communication between the client and the ResourceManager service.

A client uses this interface to:

- Create/submit/kill an application
- Get reports for application/container/application attempts
- Get information related to cluster metrics/nodes/queues

- Use filters to fetch application and nodes list (`GetApplicationsRequest` and `GetClusterNodesRequest`)
- Request for a new delegation token or renew the existing one

ApplicationMasterProtocol

The `ApplicationMasterProtocol` interface is used by an active ApplicationMaster instance to communicate with the ResourceManager service. As soon as an ApplicationMaster service gets started, it registers itself to the ResourceManager. The ApplicationMaster instance sends `AllocateRequest` to the ResourceManager to request for new containers and releases unused or blacklisted containers. After application execution, the ApplicationMaster sends a notification to the ResourceManager using the `finishApplicationMaster()` method.

ContainerManagementProtocol

The `ContainerManagementProtocol` interface is used as a communication protocol between an active ApplicationMaster and NodeManager service. The ResourceManager service allocates containers to an ApplicationMaster instance and the ApplicationMaster then submits a start container request to the corresponding NodeManager.

An active ApplicationMaster uses this interface to:

- Request NodeManager to start containers using `ContainerLaunchContext` for each container
- Get the current status of the containers
- Stop the containers corresponding to specified container IDs

ApplicationHistoryProtocol

`ApplicationHistoryProtocol` is a new protocol added in the 2.5 version of Hadoop. This protocol is used for communication between clients and the application history server (Timeline server) to fetch information related to completed applications. A Timeline server keeps the historical data for applications submitted to the YARN cluster. A client can use this interface to get reports for competed applications, containers, and application attempts.

To read more about the available communication protocols, you can refer to the Hadoop API documentation at `http://hadoop.apache.org/docs/r2.5.1/api/org/apache/hadoop/yarn/api/package-summary.html`.

YARN client API

YARN client API refers to the classes defined in the `org.apache.hadoop.yarn.client.api` package. These classes use the earlier mentioned communication protocols and are used while writing Java-based YARN applications. These are the classes exposed to a client / ApplicationMaster service to communicate with YARN daemons.

Some of the classes in the client API are:

- `YarnClient`: This is a communication bridge between the client and the ResourceManager service. A client can submit an application, request application status/report and get cluster metrics.

- `AMRMClient` / `AMRMClientAsync`: These facilitate blocking `AMRMClient` and non-blocking `AMRMClientAsync` communication between ApplicationMaster and the ResourceManager. As mentioned in *Chapter 5*, *Understanding YARN Life Cycle Management*, the ApplicationMaster connects to the ResourceManager service using `AMRMClient`. The ApplicationMaster uses the `AMRMClient` to register the AM service, to request resources from ResourceManager, and to get the resource availability of the cluster.

- `NMClient` / `NMClientAsync`: These facilitate blocking `NMClient` and non-blocking `NMClientAsync` communication between ApplicationMaster and the NodeManager. Similar to a connection to ResourceManager, the ApplicationMaster creates a connection to the NodeManager on which containers are allocated. The ApplicationMaster uses the `NMClient` to request start/stop containers and get container status.

- `AHSClient` / `TimelineClient`: This facilitate communication between client and Timeline server. Once the applications are completed, a client can fetch the application report from the Timeline sever. The client uses the `AHSClient` to get the list of applications, application attempts, and containers.

To read more about the YARN client API, you can refer to the Hadoop API documentation at `http://hadoop.apache.org/docs/r2.5.1/api/org/apache/hadoop/yarn/client/api/package-summary.html`.

Writing your own application

YARN framework provides flexibility to run any application in a clustered environment. An application could be as simple as a Java process, a shell script, or a simple date command. The ResourceManager service manages the cluster resource allocation and the NodeManager services execute tasks as specified by the application framework; for example, the map and reduce tasks of Hadoop MapReduce jobs.

In this section, you will write your own applications to run in a distributed environment through YARN.

The complete process can be summarized in four simple steps, which are shown in the following diagram:

Step 1 – Create a new project and add Hadoop-YARN JAR files

We will create a new Java project in Eclipse and will use the YARN client APIs to write a simple YARN application. You can either create a simple Java project or a Maven project.

You need to add the following jar files to your project's build path:

- `hadoop-yarn-client-2.5.1.jar`
- `hadoop-yarn-api-2.5.1.jar`
- `hadoop-yarn-common-2.5.1.jar`
- `hadoop-common-2.5.1.jar`

If you choose to create a simple Java project, you can create a library folder (named `lib`) to store the required `jar` files in your project directory and add the required `jar` files to the library folder. If you choose to create a Maven project, then you will need to add the following dependency entries in `pom.xml` and install the project to resolve the dependencies:

```
<dependency>
  <groupId>org.apache.hadoop</groupId>
  <artifactId>hadoop-yarn-client</artifactId>
  <version>2.5.1</version>
</dependency>

<dependency>
  <groupId>org.apache.hadoop</groupId>
  <artifactId>hadoop-yarn-common</artifactId>
  <version>2.5.1</version>
</dependency>

<dependency>
  <groupId>org.apache.hadoop</groupId>
  <artifactId>hadoop-yarn-api</artifactId>
  <version>2.5.1</version>
</dependency>

<dependency>
  <groupId>org.apache.hadoop</groupId>
  <artifactId>hadoop-common</artifactId>
  <version>2.5.1</version>
</dependency>
```

Step 2 – Define the ApplicationMaster and client classes

A client needs to define classes for ApplicationMaster to manage the application execution and YARN client to submit the application to ResourceManager.

The following are the roles for client while writing the ApplicationMaster and YARN client:

Define an Application Master	Initialize AMRMClient and NMClient clients
	Register the attempt with the ResourceManager
	Define ContainerRequest and add containers request
	Request allocation, define ContainerLaunchContext and start containers
	On completion, unregister ApplicationMaster from RM
Submit application to Resource Manager	Read YARNConfiguration and initialize YARNClient
	Connect to RM and request for new application id
	Define ContainerLaunchContext for Application Master
	Create ApplicationSubmissionContext
	Submit application and wait for completion

Define an ApplicationMaster

Create a new package and add a new class `ApplicationMaster.java` with the main method to your project. You need to add the following code snippets to the `ApplicationMaster.java` class:

```
package com.packt.firstyarnapp;

import java.util.Collections;

import org.apache.hadoop.conf.Configuration;
import org.apache.hadoop.net.NetUtils;
import org.apache.hadoop.yarn.api.ApplicationConstants;
import org.apache.hadoop.yarn.api.protocolrecords.AllocateResponse;
import org.apache.hadoop.yarn.api.records.Container;
import org.apache.hadoop.yarn.api.records.ContainerLaunchContext;
import org.apache.hadoop.yarn.api.records.ContainerStatus;
import org.apache.hadoop.yarn.api.records.FinalApplicationStatus;
import org.apache.hadoop.yarn.api.records.Priority;
import org.apache.hadoop.yarn.api.records.Resource;
```

```
import org.apache.hadoop.yarn.client.api.AMRMClient;

import org.apache.hadoop.yarn.client.api.AMRMClient.ContainerRequest;

import org.apache.hadoop.yarn.client.api.NMClient;

import org.apache.hadoop.yarn.conf.YarnConfiguration;

import org.apache.hadoop.yarn.util.Records;


public class ApplicationMaster {

  public static void main(String[] args) throws Exception {
    System.out.println("Running ApplicationMaster");
    final String shellCommand = args[0];
    final int numOfContainers = Integer.valueOf(args[1]);
    Configuration conf = new YarnConfiguration();

    // Point #2
    System.out.println("Initializing AMRMCLient");
    AMRMClient<ContainerRequest> rmClient = AMRMClient.
createAMRMClient();
    rmClient.init(conf);
    rmClient.start();

    System.out.println("Initializing NMCLient");
    NMClient nmClient = NMClient.createNMClient();
    nmClient.init(conf);
    nmClient.start();

    // Point #3
    System.out.println("Register ApplicationMaster");
    rmClient.registerApplicationMaster(NetUtils.getHostname(), 0, "");

    // Point #4
    Priority priority = Records.newRecord(Priority.class);
    priority.setPriority(0);
```

```
System.out.println("Setting Resource capability for Containers");
Resource capability = Records.newRecord(Resource.class);
capability.setMemory(128);
capability.setVirtualCores(1);
for (int i = 0; i < numOfContainers; ++i) {
  ContainerRequest containerRequested = new ContainerRequest(
      capability, null, null, priority, true);
  // Resource, nodes, racks, priority and relax locality flag
  rmClient.addContainerRequest(containerRequested);
}


// Point #6
int allocatedContainers = 0;
System.out
    .println("Requesting container allocation from ResourceManager");
while (allocatedContainers < numOfContainers) {
  AllocateResponse response = rmClient.allocate(0);
  for (Container container : response.getAllocatedContainers()) {
    ++allocatedContainers;
    // Launch container by creating ContainerLaunchContext
    ContainerLaunchContext ctx = Records
        .newRecord(ContainerLaunchContext.class);
    ctx.setCommands(Collections.singletonList(shellCommand + " 1>"
        + ApplicationConstants.LOG_DIR_EXPANSION_VAR
        + "/stdout" + " 2>"
        + ApplicationConstants.LOG_DIR_EXPANSION_VAR
        + "/stderr"));
    System.out.println("Starting container on node : "
        + container.getNodeHttpAddress());
    nmClient.startContainer(container, ctx);
  }
  Thread.sleep(100);
}
```

```
// Point #6

int completedContainers = 0;

while (completedContainers < numOfContainers) {

    AllocateResponse response = rmClient.allocate(completedContainers
        / numOfContainers);


    for (ContainerStatus status : response
        .getCompletedContainersStatuses()) {

      ++completedContainers;

      System.out.println("Container completed : " + status.
getContainerId())
;

      System.out
            .println("Completed container " + completedContainers);

    }

    Thread.sleep(100);

  }

  rmClient.unregisterApplicationMaster(FinalApplicationStatus.
SUCCEEDED,

      "", "");


  }


}
```

The code snippets of the ApplicationMaster are explained as follows:

1. **Read YARN configuration and input arguments**: The ApplicationMaster uses the YARNConfiguration class to load the Hadoop-YARN configuration files and reads the specified input arguments. For this example, the first argument is a shellCommand such as /bin/date and the second argument is the numofContainers to be launched during application execution:

   ```
   Public static void main(String[] args) throws Exception {

       final String shellCommand = args[0];

       final intnumOfContainers = Integer.valueOf(args[1]);

       Configuration conf = new YarnConfiguration();

   }
   ```

2. **Initialize the AMRMClient and NMClient clients**: The ApplicationMaster first creates and initializes the communication interfaces with the ResourceManager service AMRMClient and the NodeManager service NMClient as given in the following code:

```
AMRMClient<ContainerRequest> rmClient =
AMRMClient.createAMRMClient();

rmClient.init(conf);

rmClient.start();


NMClient nmClient = NMClient.createNMClient();

nmClient.init(conf);

nmClient.start();
```

3. **Register the attempt with the ResourceManager**: The ApplicationMaster registers itself to the ResourceManager service. It needs to specify the hostname, port and a tracking URL for the attempt. After successful registration, the ResourceManager moves the application state to RUNNING.

```
rmClient.registerApplicationMaster(NetUtils.getHostname(), 0,
"");
```

4. **Define ContainerRequest and add the container's request**: The client defines the execution requirement of worker containers in terms of memory and cores (org.apache.hadoop.yarn.api.records.Resource). The client might also specify the priority of the worker containers, a preferred list of nodes, and racks for resource locality. The client creates a ContainerRequest reference and adds the requests before calling the allocate() method:

```
Priority priority = Records.newRecord(Priority.class);

priority.setPriority(0);


Resource capability = Records.newRecord(Resource.class);

capability.setMemory(128);

capability.setVirtualCores(1);

for (inti = 0; i<numOfContainers; ++i) {

ContainerRequest containerRequested = new
ContainerRequest(capability, null, null, priority, true);

// Resource, nodes, racks, priority and relax locality flag

rmClient.addContainerRequest(containerRequested);

}
```

5. **Request allocation, define ContainerLaunchContext and start the containers**: The ApplicationMaster requests the ResourceManager to allocate the required containers and notifies the ResourceManager about the current progress of the application. Hence, the value of progress indicator during the first allocation request is 0. The response from the ResourceManager contains the number of allocated containers. The ApplicationMaster creates `ContainerLaunchContext` for each allocated container and requests the corresponding NodeManager to start the container. It will wait for the execution of the containers. In this example, the command executed to launch the containers is specified as the first argument for the ApplicationMaster (the `/bin/date` command):

```
intallocatedContainers = 0;
    while (allocatedContainers<numOfContainers) {
AllocateResponse response = rmClient.allocate(0);
      for (Container container :
response.getAllocatedContainers()) {
      ++allocatedContainers;
      // Launch container by creating ContainerLaunchContext
      ContainerLaunchContext ctx =
Records.newRecord(ContainerLaunchContext.class);
ctx.setCommands(Collections.singletonList(shellCommand +
" 1>" + ApplicationConstants.LOG_DIR_EXPANSION_VAR + "/stdout"
+
" 2>" + ApplicationConstants.LOG_DIR_EXPANSION_VAR + "/stderr"
            ));
nmClient.startContainer(container, ctx);
}
Thread.sleep(100);
}
```

6. **On completion, unregister ApplicationMaster from ResourceManager**: The allocation response also contains the list of completed containers. Once all the containers acquired in the response start executing on the different NodeManagers, the ApplicationMaster waits for its completion. The `ContainerStatus` class provides the current status of the containers in execution. To unregister ApplicationMaster, call the `unregisterApplicationMaster()` method on the `AMRMClient` reference. With the unregister call, the ApplicationMaster sends the final status of the application, application message, and final application tracking URL as arguments:

```
intcompletedContainers = 0;
    while (completedContainers<numOfContainers) {
```

```
AllocateResponse response =
rmClient.allocate(completedContainers/numOfContainers);


    for (ContainerStatus status :
response.getCompletedContainersStatuses()) {

        ++completedContainers;
System.out.println("Completed container " +
completedContainers);
            }
Thread.sleep(100);
    }


rmClient.unregisterApplicationMaster(FinalApplicationStatus.SU
CCEEDED, "", "");
```

Define a YARN client

Add a new class `Client.java` with the main method to your project. For simplicity, you can create it within the same project.

The code for the `Client.java` file is as follows:

```
package com.packt.firstyarnapp;


import java.io.File;
import java.util.Collections;
import java.util.HashMap;
import java.util.Map;


import org.apache.hadoop.fs.FileStatus;
import org.apache.hadoop.fs.FileSystem;
import org.apache.hadoop.fs.Path;
import org.apache.hadoop.yarn.api.ApplicationConstants;
import org.apache.hadoop.yarn.api.ApplicationConstants.Environment;
import org.apache.hadoop.yarn.api.records.ApplicationId;
import org.apache.hadoop.yarn.api.records.ApplicationReport;
import
org.apache.hadoop.yarn.api.records.ApplicationSubmissionContex
t;
```

```
import
org.apache.hadoop.yarn.api.records.ContainerLaunchContext;
import org.apache.hadoop.yarn.api.records.LocalResource;
import org.apache.hadoop.yarn.api.records.LocalResourceType;
import
org.apache.hadoop.yarn.api.records.LocalResourceVisibility;
import org.apache.hadoop.yarn.api.records.Resource;
import
org.apache.hadoop.yarn.api.records.YarnApplicationState;
import org.apache.hadoop.yarn.client.api.YarnClient;
import
org.apache.hadoop.yarn.client.api.YarnClientApplication;
import org.apache.hadoop.yarn.conf.YarnConfiguration;
import org.apache.hadoop.yarn.util.Apps;
import org.apache.hadoop.yarn.util.ConverterUtils;
import org.apache.hadoop.yarn.util.Records;

public class Client {

  public static void main(String[] args) throws Exception {
    try {
      Client clientObj = new Client();
      if (clientObj.run(args)) {
        System.out.println("Application completed
successfully");
      } else {
        System.out.println("Application Failed / Killed");
      }
    } catch (Exception e) {
      e.printStackTrace();
    }
  }

  public boolean run(String[] args) throws Exception {
    // Point #1
    final String command = args[0];
    final int n = Integer.valueOf(args[1]);
    final Path jarPath = new Path(args[2]);
```

```
    System.out.println("Initializing YARN configuration");

    YarnConfiguration conf = new YarnConfiguration();

    YarnClient yarnClient = YarnClient.createYarnClient();

    yarnClient.init(conf);

    yarnClient.start();


    // Point #2

    System.out.println("Requesting ResourceManager for a new
Application");

    YarnClientApplication app =
yarnClient.createApplication();


    // Point #3

    System.out.println("Initializing ContainerLaunchContext
for ApplicationMaster container");

    ContainerLaunchContext amContainer = Records
        .newRecord(ContainerLaunchContext.class);


    System.out.println("Adding LocalResource");

    LocalResource appMasterJar =
Records.newRecord(LocalResource.class);

    FileStatus jarStat = FileSystem.get(conf).getFileStatus(jarPath);

appMasterJar.setResource(ConverterUtils.getYarnUrlFromPath(jar
Path));

    appMasterJar.setSize(jarStat.getLen());

    appMasterJar.setTimestamp(jarStat.getModificationTime());

    appMasterJar.setType(LocalResourceType.FILE);

    appMasterJar.setVisibility(LocalResourceVisibility.PUBLIC);


    // Point #4

    System.out.println("Setting environment");

    Map<String, String> appMasterEnv = new HashMap<String,
String>();

    for (String c : conf.getStrings(
        YarnConfiguration.YARN_APPLICATION_CLASSPATH,
        YarnConfiguration.DEFAULT_YARN_APPLICATION_CLASSPATH))
    {
```

```
    Apps.addToEnvironment(appMasterEnv,
Environment.CLASSPATH.name(),
        c.trim());
    }

    Apps.addToEnvironment(appMasterEnv,
Environment.CLASSPATH.name(),
        Environment.PWD.$() + File.separator + "*");

    System.out.println("Setting resource capability");
    Resource capability = Records.newRecord(Resource.class);
    capability.setMemory(256);
    capability.setVirtualCores(1);

    System.out.println("Setting command to start
ApplicationMaster service");
    amContainer.setCommands(Collections.singletonList("/usr/lib/jv
m/jdk1.8.0/bin/java"
        + " -Xmx256M" + "
com.packt.firstyarnapp.ApplicationMaster"
        + " " + command + " " + String.valueOf(n) + " 1>"
        + ApplicationConstants.LOG_DIR_EXPANSION_VAR +
"/stdout"
        + " 2>" + ApplicationConstants.LOG_DIR_EXPANSION_VAR
        + "/stderr"));
    amContainer.setLocalResources(Collections.singletonMap(
        "first-yarn-app.jar", appMasterJar));
    amContainer.setEnvironment(appMasterEnv);

    System.out.println("Initializing
ApplicationSubmissionContext");
    ApplicationSubmissionContext appContext = app
        .getApplicationSubmissionContext();
    appContext.setApplicationName("first-yarn-app");
    appContext.setApplicationType("YARN");
    appContext.setAMContainerSpec(amContainer);
    appContext.setResource(capability);
    appContext.setQueue("default");
```

```
    ApplicationId appId = appContext.getApplicationId();

    System.out.println("Submitting application " + appId);

    yarnClient.submitApplication(appContext);


    ApplicationReport appReport =
yarnClient.getApplicationReport(appId);
    YarnApplicationState appState =
appReport.getYarnApplicationState();
    while (appState != YarnApplicationState.FINISHED

        && appState != YarnApplicationState.KILLED

        && appState != YarnApplicationState.FAILED) {

    Thread.sleep(100);

    appReport = yarnClient.getApplicationReport(appId);

    appState = appReport.getYarnApplicationState();

    }
    if (appState == YarnApplicationState.FINISHED) {

    return true;

    } else {

    return false;

    }

  }

}
```

You need to add the code snippets given in the following steps to the `run()` method of the `Client.java` class:

1. **Read YARNConfiguration and initialize YARNClient**: Similar to the ApplicationMaster, the client also uses the `YARNConfiguration` class to load the Hadoop-YARN configuration files and reads the specified input arguments. The client initiates a `YARNClient` service on the client node.

   In this example, the first two arguments are directly passed to the `ContainerLaunchContext` of ApplicationMaster and the third argument is the HDFS path for job resources (`jar` file with ApplicationMaster):

   ```
   public Booleanrun(String[] args) throws Exception {
   final String command = args[0];
       final int n = Integer.valueOf(args[1]);
       final Path jarPath = new Path(args[2]);
   ```

```
YarnConfigurationconf = new YarnConfiguration();

YarnClientyarnClient=YarnClient.createYarnClient();

yarnClient.init(conf);

yarnClient.start();
}
```

2. **Connect to ResourceManager and request for a new application ID**:
   The client connects to the ResourceManager service and requests a new
   application. The response of the request (that is, `YarnClientApplication`
   – `GetNewApplicationResponse`) contains a new application ID and the
   minimum and maximum resource capability of the cluster.

   ```
   YarnClientApplication app = yarnClient.createApplication();
   ```

3. **Define ContainerLaunchContext for Application Master**: The first container
   for an application is the ApplicationMaster's container. The client defines
   a `ContainerLaunchContext`, which contains information to start the
   ApplicationMaster service.

   The `ContainerLaunchContext` will contain the following information:

   ○ **Set up jar for ApplicationMaster**: The NodeManager should be
     able to locate the ApplicationMaster `jar` file. The `jar` file is placed
     on HDFS and is accessed by NodeManager as a `LocalResource` as
     given in the following code:

     ```
     ContainerLaunchContextamContainer =
     Records.newRecord(ContainerLaunchContext.class);


     LocalResourceappMasterJar =
     Records.newRecord(LocalResource.class);

     FileStatusjarStat =
     FileSystem.get(conf).getFileStatus(jarPath);

     appMasterJar.setResource(ConverterUtils.
     getYarnUrlFromPath(jar
     Path));

     appMasterJar.setSize(jarStat.getLen());

     appMasterJar.setTimestamp(jarStat.getModificationTime());
     appMasterJar.setType(LocalResourceType.FILE);

     appMasterJar.setVisibility(LocalResourceVisibility.PUBLIC);
     ```

- ∘ **Set up CLASSPATH for ApplicationMaster**: It might be possible for your shell command to run ApplicationMaster, which requires some environment variables. A client can specify a list of environment variables.

```
Map<String, String>appMasterEnv = new HashMap<String,
String>();

for (String c
:conf.getStrings(YarnConfiguration.YARN_APPLICATION_
CLASSPATH,
YarnConfiguration.DEFAULT_YARN_APPLICATION_CLASSPATH))
{
Apps.addToEnvironment(appMasterEnv,
Environment.CLASSPATH.name(),c.trim());
}
Apps.addToEnvironment(appMasterEnv,Environment.CLASSPATH.
name(
),Environment.PWD.$() + File.separator + "*");
```

- ∘ **Set up resource requirement for ApplicationMaster**: The resource requirement is defined as the memory and CPU cores required by the ApplicationMaster.

```
Resource capability = Records.newRecord(Resource.class);

capability.setMemory(256);

capability.setVirtualCores(1);
```

- ∘ **The command to start the ApplicationMaster service**: In this example, the ApplicationMaster is a Java program, so the client will define a Java `jar` command to start the ApplicationMaster.

```
amContainer.setCommands(Collections.singletonList("$JAVA_
HOME/
bin/java" +" -Xmx256M" +"
com.packt.firstyarnapp.ApplicationMaster" + " " + command +
"
" + String.valueOf(n) + " 1>" +
ApplicationConstants.LOG_DIR_EXPANSION_VAR + "/stdout" + "
2>"
+ ApplicationConstants.LOG_DIR_EXPANSION_VAR + "/stderr" ));

amContainer.setLocalResources(Collections.
singletonMap("first-
yarn-app.jar",appMasterJar));

amContainer.setEnvironment(appMasterEnv);
```

4. **Create ApplicationSubmissionContext**: The client defines
`ApplicationSubmissionContext` for the application. The submission
context contains information such as application name, queue, priority, and
so on.

```
ApplicationSubmissionContextappContext =
app.getApplicationSubmissionContext();

appContext.setApplicationName("first-yarn-app");

appContext.setApplicationType("YARN");

appContext.setAMContainerSpec(amContainer);

appContext.setResource(capability);

appContext.setQueue("default");
```

5. **Submit the application and wait for completion**: The client submits
the application and waits for application completion. It requests the
ResourceManager for the application status.

```
ApplicationIdappId = appContext.getApplicationId();

System.out.println("Submitting application " + appId);

yarnClient.submitApplication(appContext);


ApplicationReportappReport =
yarnClient.getApplicationReport(appId);

YarnApplicationStateappState =
appReport.getYarnApplicationState();

while (appState != YarnApplicationState.FINISHED&&

appState != YarnApplicationState.KILLED&&

appState != YarnApplicationState.FAILED) {

Thread.sleep(100);

appReport = yarnClient.getApplicationReport(appId);

appState = appReport.getYarnApplicationState();

}
```

Step 3 – Export the project and copy resources

You need to export the Java project as a `jar` file and copy the `jar` file on HDFS. If
you have created two different projects for `Client.java` and `ApplicationMaster.`
`java`, then you will need to export both the projects as `jar` files and copy only the
ApplicationMaster `jar` to HDFS. In this case, you need create only one `jar` file.

To copy the file to HDFS, you can use the Hadoop `hdfs` command using either the `put` or `copyFromLocal` option. Assuming the name of the `jar` to be `first-yarn-app.jar`, the `hdfs` command will look like this:

```
bin/hdfsdfs -put first-yarn-app.jar /user/hduser/first-yarn-app.jar
```

Step 4 – Run the application using bin or the YARN command

The last step is to submit the application to YARN using the `yarn` command found in Hadoop-bin folder (`$HADOOP_PREFIX/bin`).

As mentioned in the main method of the `Client.java` class, you need to pass three arguments:

- The `shell` command
- The number of containers required
- The HDFS path for the `jar` file containing ApplicationMaster

The `yarn` command will look like this:

```
bin/yarn jar first-yarn-app.jar com.packt.firstyarnapp.Client
/bin/true1 hdfs://master:8020/user/hduser/first-yarn-app.jar
```

The output of the preceding application looks like this:

```
Initializing YARN configuration

15/07/05 23:52:51 INFO client.RMProxy: Connecting to ResourceManager
at master/192.168.56.101:8032

Requesting ResourceManager for a new Application

Initializing ContainerLaunchContext for ApplicationMaster container

Adding LocalResource

Setting environment

Setting resource capability

Setting command to start ApplicationMaster service

Initializing ApplicationSubmissionContext

Submitting application application_1436101688138_0009

15/07/05 23:52:53 INFO impl.YarnClientImpl: Submitted application
application_1436101688138_0009

Application completed successfully
```

The output of the program will be displayed on the terminal. You can also refer to the ResourceManager web UI to check the status of the submitted application. As shown in the following screenshot:

> Writing a complete YARN-compatible distributed application is a very complex task and it does not allow developers to focus on the business logic. A developer/admin also needs to monitor and manage the running applications. To reduce the complexity and allow easy integration with YARN, Apache Slider and Apache Twill are two projects that are currently in incubator state. To read more about these frameworks, you can refer to their official websites at `http://slider.incubator.apache.org/` and `http://twill.incubator.apache.org/`.

Summary

Writing your own Hadoop-YARN applications allows Hadoop users to apply their own business logic (other than MapReduce programming) in a distributed environment. This chapter covered the basics of the YARN APIs and walked you through how to write a simple YARN application. To read more about the topic, you can refer to the Hadoop documentation at `http://hadoop.apache.org/docs/r2.5.1/hadoop-yarn/hadoop-yarn-site/WritingYarnApplications.html`.

The Hadoop documentation covers a bird's eye view of the APIs used while writing YARN applications. You can also refer to a sample Hortonworks project on GitHub at `https://github.com/apache/hadoop-common/tree/trunk/hadoop-yarn-project/hadoop-yarn/hadoop-yarn-applications/hadoop-yarn-applications-distributedshell`. You can build and execute it on a Hadoop-YARN cluster.

The next chapter covers YARN insights and the core services related to YARN components. It'll help the Java developers and open source contributors to understand the communication between YARN components and to dive deeper into YARN's architecture.

8
Dive Deep into YARN Components

YARN consists of various efficient and scalable components that make it a powerful, robust, and preferable resource management framework. In order to have a better understanding of YARN offerings and how to integrate YARN, users need to have in-depth knowledge of various YARN components. This chapter explains the internals of YARN components, the classes involved, and how YARN components interact with each other. The component's insights provided in this chapter will enable users to leverage the features of YARN and integrate YARN with distributed application frameworks easily.

In this chapter, we will cover the following topics:

- Understanding ResourceManager
- Understanding NodeManager
- Working with auxiliary services, resource localization, log aggregation
- An overview of Timeline server, web application proxy, and YARN scheduler load simulator

Understanding ResourceManager

ResourceManager is the core component of the YARN framework, which is responsible for managing the resources of a multinode cluster. It facilitates the resources allocation and bookkeeping for a distributed application running across multiple nodes of a YARN cluster. It works with a per node daemon called NodeManager and a per application service called ApplicationMaster. It manages resources across the cluster and executes YARN applications.

ResourceManager has several subcomponents that assist it in the efficient management of a multinodes cluster with thousands of distributed, resource exhaustive and time-bound applications running in parallel. This is shown in the following figure:

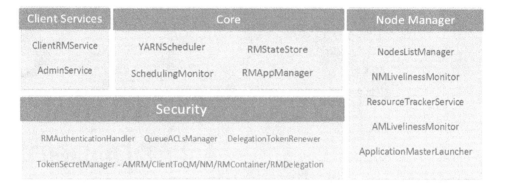

The client and admin interfaces

ResourceManager exposes methods to clients and cluster administrators for RPC communications to the ResourceManager and for accepting admin commands on priority. Here are the two classes that are used for communication to ResourceManager:

1. ClientRMService

   The `ClientRMService` class is the client interface to the ResourceManager. All clients create RPC connections to the ResourceManager. This module handles all the RPC interfaces to the ResourceManager. The implementation of this service is defined in the `org.apache.hadoop.yarn.server.resourcemanager.ClientRMService` package. Clients initialize this service using the client configuration files such as `yarn-site.xml`.

   Clients request ResourceManager for:

   ° **Application requests**: This interface exposes services such as new application requests, submitting applications to the cluster, killing an application, listing containers, fetching the application, and application attempt reports, and so on to the clients.

   ° **Cluster metrics**: The clients can also request ResourceManager to share the cluster metrics, node capabilities, scheduler details, and so on using this service.

   ° **Security**: To connect to a secured cluster environment, clients use delegation tokens and access the control lists provided by ResourceManager.

To read more about different methods defined in `ClientRMService`, you can refer to the grepcode site at `http://grepcode.com/file/ repo1.maven.org/maven2/org.apache.hadoop/hadoop-yarn- server-resourcemanager/2.6.0/org/apache/hadoop/yarn/server/ resourcemanager/ClientRMService.java`.

2. AdminService

   The `AdminService` class is used by the cluster administrators to manage the ResourceManager service. Cluster administrators use command-line options for the `rmadmin` command that internally uses `AdminService`.

   The following is the list of actions a cluster administrator can perform through `AdminService`:

   ○ Refresh the cluster nodes, access control lists and queues

   ○ Check cluster health

   ○ Manage the High Availability feature for ResourceManager.

   The implementation of this service is defined in `org.apache.hadoop.yarn. server.resourcemanager.AdminService` package.

   You can refer to the `rmadmin` command in *Chapter 3*, *Administering a Hadoop-YARN Cluster*.

The core interfaces

The ResourceManager core consists of the scheduler and applications manager. The following classes define how ResourceManager performs scheduling and manages application and state information.

1. YarnScheduler

   The `YarnScheduler` class is responsible for resource allocation and cleanup among various applications, that is, the scheduling of applications based on some predefined specifications across multiple nodes in a cluster. `YarnScheduler` is based on a pluggable policy plug-in. This plug-in is responsible for partitioning of cluster resources (CPU, memory, disk, and so on) among multiple applications, queues, and so on. It maintains a queue for scheduled applications and also has metrics of cluster resources having information such as number of nodes in the cluster, minimum and maximum resource capability, and so on. `YarnScheduler` is defined in the `org.apache. hadoop.yarn.server.resourcemanager.scheduler.YarnScheduler` interface and the two main implementations of `YarnScheduler` available with MapReduce YARN are:

   ○ Fair scheduler

      °   Capacity scheduler

A detailed explanation of schedulers and scheduler configuration is covered in *Chapter 10, Scheduling YARN Applications*.

2. RMAppManager

    `RMAppManager` is responsible for managing the list of applications for the ResourceManager executed over the YARN cluster. It runs as a service within ResourceManager. It creates and logs `ApplicationSummary`, that is, runtime information related to a particular application. The YARN client connects to this service for any application related request.

    The implementation of this service is defined in `org.apache.hadoop.yarn.server.resourcemanager.RMAppManager`.

3. RMStateStore

    To handle recovery of the ResourceManager service during failures, `RMStateStore` is an abstract implementation to store the state information of the ResourceManager service. It also stores information related to running applications and their attempts.

    Currently, YARN defines four mechanisms to store the ResourceManager state:

          °   `FileSystemRMStateStore`

          °   `MemoryRMStateStore`

          °   `ZKRMStateStore`

          °   `NullRMStateStore`

    `ZKRMStateStore` is the most reliable and recommended mechanism to store the `RMState`, but it requires a Zookeeper ensemble to store the information as `Znode`. The state store mechanism in ResourceManager is also used while configuring the ResourceManager High Availability feature. For more information on the state store, you can refer to the state store configurations specified in ResourceManager High Availability in *Chapter 3, Administering a Hadoop-YARN Cluster*.

4. SchedulingMonitor

    This interface provides monitoring of containers and a provision to edit schedules at regular intervals. It also provides provision to tune the monitor interval of resources and to define `SchedulingEditPolicy`. To read more about `SchedulingMonitor`, you can refer to the `org.apache.hadoop.yarn.server.resourcemanager.monitor.SchedulingMonitor` class.

The NodeManager interfaces

The ResourceManager service communicates with the NodeManager service. The NodeManager service sends regular updates to the ResourceManager service containing the health and resource information of the node. Here are a few classes of ResourceManager that manages the NodeManager nodes across the cluster:

1. NMLivelinessMonitor

   `NMLivelinessMonitor` helps ResourceManager to keep track of all live NodeManager nodes in the cluster and more importantly, the unusable ones in the system. It receives heartbeats frequently from all NodeManager nodes and considers a node to be dead if it does not receive any heartbeats for 600,000 milliseconds or 10 minutes (default). This interval could be configured through the `RM_NM_EXPIRY_INTERVAL_MS` property of YARN configuration. When a node is marked as dead, all the containers running on that node is also considered to be dead and no new container will be scheduled on that node. The ResourceManager reallocates resources for the containers running on that dead node.

   To override the default value of the expiry interval, an administrator can configure the following property in the `yarn-site.xml` file:

   ```
   <property>
       <name>yarn.am.liveness-monitor.expiry-interval-ms</name>
       <value>600000</value>
   </property>
   ```

   The implementation of this service is defined in `org.apache.hadoop.yarn.server.resourcemanager.NMLivelinessMonitor`.

2. ApplicationMasterLauncher

   `ApplicationMasterLauncher` maintains a queue of application masters for different applications submitted to the YARN cluster. It launches an AM as a service, taking one application at a time from the queue. It also maintains a thread-pool to launch AMs and cleaning up AMs when the application is finished or terminated forcefully. The implementation of this service is defined in `org.apache.hadoop.yarn.server.resourcemanager.amlauncher.ApplicationMasterLauncher`.

The security and token managers

ResourceManager manages a set of tokens for authentication and authorization of different RPC communication channels. ResourceManager manages the services explained in the upcoming sections for security.

1. RMAuthenticationHandler

   RMAuthenticationHandler is responsible for authenticating a request based on the delegation header and then returning a valid token for that request. It extends the KerberosAuthenticationHandler class and is used when Kerberos security is enabled.

   Kerberos is an authentication protocol used to authenticate the identity of the services running and communicating on different nodes over a nonsecure network. An overview of Kerberos and YARN Kerberos configurations is covered in *Chapter 11, Enabling Security in YARN*. To read more about this service, you can refer to the org.apache.hadoop.yarn.server. resourcemanager.security.RMAuthenticationHandler package.

2. QueueACLsManager

   The YarnScheduler uses the QueueACLsManager class to check whether a user has access to a particular queue. If the ACLs are not enabled, then it'll allow all users to submit applications to all queues. A detailed explanation on queues and queue ACLs is given in *Chapter 10, Scheduling YARN Applications* and *Chapter 11, Enabling Security in YARN*.

3. TokenSecretManagers for RM

   ResourceManager defines TokenSecretManagers to manage security across multiple applications, containers, and nodes.

   Few of the TokenSecretManagers are:

   - AMRMTokenSecretManager
   - ClientToAMTokenSecretManagerInRM
   - NMTokenSecretManagerInRM
   - RMContainerTokenSecretManager
   - RMDelegationTokenSecretManager

Understanding NodeManager

The NodeManager node is the worker node for YARN and is responsible for updating the resource availability on a node to ResourceManager. It is also responsible for monitoring the health of a node and for executing containers for an application.

The following diagram shows various subcomponents of the NodeManager daemon followed by a detailed description of these subcomponents:

Status Updates	State and Health Management		Security
NodeManagerMetrics	NMStateStoreService	NodeHealthCheckerService	NMTokenSecretManagerInNM
NodeStatusUpdater	LocalDirsHandlerService	NodeHealthScriptRunner	NMContainerTokenSecretManager

Container Management			
ContainersLauncher	ContainerManager	ContainerExecutor	AuxServices
ContainersMonitor	ContainerLocalization	ContainerLocalizer	LogAggregationService

Status updates

The resource capability of a cluster is calculated as the sum of the capabilities of all NodeManager nodes. To utilize cluster resources efficiently, it is important to keep track of all resources across the cluster. NodeManager nodes send regular status updates to the ResourceManager. This enables ResourceManager to schedule execution of applications efficiently and increases the cluster performance. Few of the classes defined in the NodeManager framework for sending updates are mentioned in the upcoming sections.

1. NodeStatusUpdater

   Every slave node with the NodeManager daemon registers itself with ResourceManager. The NodeManager daemon specifies its resource capability to the ResourceManager. It has a `StatusUpdater` service, which updates the node's current status with respect to applications and containers running on it.

   It computes resource capability in terms of:

   ° Physical memory

   ° Virtual to physical memory ratio

   ° Number of cores

   ° Duration to track stopped containers

   It exposes public interfaces to request and update the container's current status. The implementation of this service is defined in `org.apache.hadoop.yarn.server.nodemanager.NodeStatusUpdaterImpl`.

2. NodeManagerMetrics

The NodeManager daemon manages a metrics of the resources available on the Node. It stores the initial metrics for the node and updates the metrics for different events of a container such as container launch, complete, killed, and so on. The current resource metrics implementation takes memory and CPU cores into account. The implementation of this service is defined in `org.apache.hadoop.yarn.server.nodemanager.metrics.NodeManagerMetrics`.

State and health management

It is important to periodically check the health of different nodes in the cluster and take necessary action if any of the nodes are found to be unhealthy. The NodeManager service provides utilities to manage the state and monitor the health of a node at any point of time. As a part of failure/fault management and recovery, even if an unhealthy node goes out of the network or becomes faulty, NodeManager provides services to recover the state of resources on the node and again actively participate in cluster operations.

1. NodeHealthCheckerService

This service provides status on the NodeManager node's current state of health. It executes a user-defined script on the node to monitor the health of the Node using the `NodeHealthScriptRunner` service.

The script execution ends with any one of the following results:

- `SUCCESS`
- `TIMED_OUT`
- `FAILED_WITH_EXIT_CODE`
- `FAILED_WITH_EXCEPTION`
- `FAILED`

Internally, this service would only check for output of the script to be started with the `ERROR` pattern. If the service finds any match or timeout is hit during script execution, it would mark the node as unhealthy and return the report to the service asked for the report.

2. NMStateStoreService

   The NodeManager is responsible for storing the resources for containers locally. The terminology used in YARN to provide resources to containers is termed as resource localization. The NMStateStoreService service stores the state of localized and in progress resources on NodeManager at any point of time. It also provides a handle for the recovery of user's resources and localization state.

Container management

NodeManager implements different services to meet the pre-requisites for running a container and its monitoring. For example, a container may require extra resources to be downloaded for its execution or any auxiliary service needed by the container. The upcoming sections provide a detailed explanation of different services managed by NodeManager for container management:

1. ContainerExecutor

   This interface of NodeManager is responsible for fulfilling the prerequisites, including resource localization, container's directory creation (user and application specific directories and caches), and finally executing containers as requested. It also facilitates killing a container, checking whether a container is alive, and sending the signal to a container.

2. ResourceLocalizationService

   NodeManager instantiates ResourceLocalizationService to ensure locality of the resources required by the container to run the application's task. ResourceLocalizationService downloads resources corresponding to an application on NodeManager's local filesystem. Containers use these resources for execution of the application. When the execution of the container finishes, ResourceLocalizationService cleans up the resources from the disk.

3. ContainersLauncher

   The ContainersLauncher service launches the containers on the node. This service should only be started after ResourceLocalizationService as the latter creates the system directories in the local file and download any resources required by the container. This service launches the containers one by one. It receives either of the following ContainersLauncherEvent:

   ° LAUNCH_CONTAINER: If the event type is launch_container, the ContainersLauncher service launches the container using ExecuterService

    ◦ CLEANUP_CONTAINER: If the event type is cleanup_container, the ContainersLauncher service sends the signal to kill the container process and clean up the container's directories on the local filesystem

4. ContainersMonitor

   ContainersMonitor is a service to monitor containers running on a slave node. It maintains a list of containers the NodeManager needs to monitor. It adds ContainerId and ProcessTreeInfo to the list when a new container is started on the node and removes the finished containers from the list.

5. Auxiliary service

   Auxiliary service is a framework to define per node customer services required for running applications over YARN. Considering an example of a Hadoop MapReduce job, the output of map phase is to be transferred to the reducer node. The NodeManager daemon provides a handle to retrieve the metadata for the MapReduce services in Hadoop. The metadata can be the connection information between a mapper and a reducer to transfer map output files during MapReduce job execution. Hadoop provides mapreduce_shuffle as an auxiliary service for NodeManager as shown in the following figure.

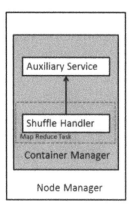

6. LogHandler and log aggregation

   LogHandler is a pluggable implementation for logging of application and containers. Nonaggregated logs are generated on the local filesystem for every application executed over YARN. Logs get deleted after the configured retention period, which, by default, is three hours, and could be configured by setting up the NM_LOG_RETAIN_SECONDS property.

YARN provides an option to consolidate the container logs generated for an application on different NodeManager nodes to a centralized location. `LogAggregationService` implemented as part of NodeManager's `ContainerManager` component run aggregators for each application running on YARN to push the logs from NodeManager nodes to HDFS.

The security and token managers

NodeManager manages the following security services:

- `NMTokenSecretManagerInNM`: This manages the keys for authentication and the authorization of NodeManager nodes and applications that are going to run on a NodeManager node.

- `NMContainerTokenSecretManager`: This manages and authenticates containers running on the NodeManager node. It checks for a key from the container with a key for the same container from ResourceManager; after successful authentication, it allows the container to run on the node.

The YARN Timeline server

It keeps the information for current and historic applications executed on the YARN cluster. It performs the following two important tasks:

- Generic information about the completed applications. It provides the following information for an application:
  - Queue name
  - User information
  - Application attempts
  - Containers that ran for every application attempt
  - Containers

- Per framework information of running and completed applications:
  - Application or framework-specific information, such as the number of map reduce tasks for a MapReduce application.
  - The user published information from client or application master.

To configure and start the YARN Timeline server, you can refer to *Chapter 3, Administering a Hadoop-YARN Cluster*.

The web application proxy server

Web application proxy server is introduced in YARN to reduce the possibility of web-based attacks through YARN. By default, it is run as part of ResourceManager but could be configured by the administrator by setting up the following property in `yarn-site.xml`.

In YARN, Application Master is responsible for providing a web UI and provides link information to ResourceManager. This causes services communication vulnerable to certain common attacks. The web application proxy mitigates the risk by warning users who do not own the given application that they are connecting to an untrusted site.

YARN Scheduler Load Simulator (SLS)

SLS is a tool that simulates load corresponds to a large scale YARN cluster in a single machine. It helps researchers and developers to prototype new scheduler features and predicts the performance and behavior over the large cluster. The size of the cluster and application load could be configured from configuration files. The simulator will produce real-time metrics for:

- Resource usage for the whole cluster and each queue
- Detailed application execution trace for analyzing scheduler behavior in terms of throughput, fairness, a job's turnaround time
- Key metrics of the scheduler algorithm, such as time of each scheduler operation

Handling resource localization in YARN

Resource is anything that is required by the container to execute the assigned task. Since the containers are running and managed by NodeManager on different nodes, it is the responsibility of NodeManager to make the required resources available on every node. YARN facilitates this feature of NodeManager by providing `ResourceLocalizationService`. This service is responsible for downloading the application resource locally to the NodeManager node's filesystem and to make it available to containers running for that application.

Resource localization terminologies

In this section, we'll discuss a few terminologies related to resource localization in YARN. In order to configure and use resource localization, it is important to understand the following concepts:

- `LocalResource`: It is defined as a resource required by the container for the execution of the application. NodeManager is responsible for making the resources available to the local filesystem before launching the container. A `LocalResource` has the following properties:

  - `URL`: The location where the resource is available and could be downloaded from.

  - `LocalResourceType`: It defines the type of resource to be downloaded by NodeManager. It is one of of the following: |

    `ARCHIVE`: NodeManager automatically decompresses archive resources.

    `FILE`

    `PATTERN`: This includes partially archived files containing a mix of archived and normal files.

  - `Size`: This is the size of the resource to be localized.

  - `Timestamp`: This is the original timestamp of the resource to be localized. It is used for verification.

  - `LocalResourceVisibility`: This specifies the visibility of the resource downloaded to the local filesystem of the NodeManager node. It is defined under:

    `PUBLIC`: This is shared by all the users on the node.

    `PRIVATE`: This is shared by all the applications of a user.

    `APPLICATION`: This is shared by all the containers running for a particular application.

- `ResourceState`: This represents the state of resource at any point of time. The valid states are:

  - `INIT`

  - `DOWNLOADING`

  - `LOCALIZED`

  - `FAILED`

- `LocalizerTracker`: This is a subcomponent of `ResourceLocalizationService`. It handles `ContainerLocalizer` spawning. It spawns and tracks private and public localizers.

- `PublicLocalizer`: This starts as a separate thread and downloads the public resource to NodeManager's node local filesystem. It also ensures safe downloading if multiple containers are requesting for the same resource at the same time by checking the state of resource against downloading the state.

- `LocalizerRunner`: This starts up as a separate process and runs `ContainerLocalizer` with access to the user's credential.

The resource localization directory structure

For resource localization, YARN creates and uses the user logs directory under Hadoop's default log directory. Users can specify a directory to be used by YARN to download and store resources, as shown in the following figure:

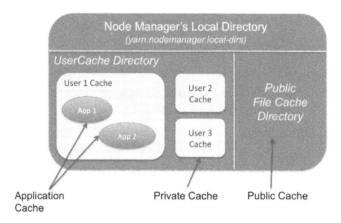

`ResourceLocalizationService` uses either the default or user defined local directory and create subdirectories for cache and resource. Depending on the resource visibility, the directories are categorized as explained in the upcoming sections:

1. Public

   Resources with public visibility are shared across all users. All the resources are placed under a single directory in the local directory of NodeManager, that is, `<yarn.nodemanager.local-dirs>/filecache` as shown in the following:

Directory Path: ***<local-dir>/filecache***

2. Private

   A resource with private visibility is shared across all the user's application. All resources are stored under the user specific cache directory, that is, `<yarn.nodemanager.local-dirs>/usercache/<username>/filecache` as shown in the following:

Directory Path: ***<local-dir>/usercache/<user-name>/***

3. Application

   A resource with application visibility is shared across all containers of an application and is stored under an application-specific cache directory, that is, `<yarn.nodemanager.local-dirs>/usercache/<username>/appcache/<appId>/` as shown in the following:

Directory Path: ***<local-dir>/usercache/<user-name>/appcache/<application-id>***

Summary

As YARN is a powerful resource management framework, it is important to know what makes it robust and efficient. An easy-to-understand and in-depth explanation of different YARN components helps users to get a clear picture of component's roles and responsibilities. This chapter also covered how YARN components communicate with each other and gave an overview of the features, including resource localization, log aggregation and auxiliary services. This chapter helps users to understand the core functionality of YARN and how it can used efficiently in various use cases.

In the next chapter, we'll explore the REST APIs exposed by different YARN services and how we can use the APIs as monitoring information.

9
Exploring YARN
REST Services

Web services based on the Representational State Transfer (REST) architectural style are called RESTful Application Programming Interfaces (APIs) or REST APIs. RESTful services use HTTP protocol as a primary protocol for communication. To read more about REST services, refer to the wiki page at `http://en.wikipedia.org/wiki/Representational_state_transfer`.

YARN defines a set of identifiers or URIs that expose information related to clusters, nodes, applications, and so on, through REST APIs. This chapter covers the list of REST APIs defined for different YARN daemons and the different ways to access REST services.

In this chapter, we will cover the following topics:

- Introduction to YARN REST services
- ResourceManager REST APIs
- NodeManager REST APIs
- MapReduce ApplicationMaster REST APIs
- MapReduce HistoryServer REST APIs
- How to access REST services data

Introduction to YARN REST services

All YARN daemons expose a set of URIs as REST APIs to fetch cluster information. The format for a URI representing a REST API is as follows:

```
http://{http address of service}/ws/{version}/{resourcepath}
```

It consists of the following three placeholders:

- `http address of service`: This is a set of the host name (or IP address) and HTTP port for a YARN service or a DNS mapping to host and port, if hosted publically. For example, the HTTP address of a REST API for ResourceManager with host name `master` and HTTP port `8088` will be `master:8088`.

- `version`: This is the latest version number for the APIs defined by YARN services. The current version of YARN services is `v1`.

- `resourcepath`: This path is uniquely resolved to a resource at the server. For example, the value of a resource path defined to fetch cluster metrics is `cluster/metrics`.

Hence, a sample URI for the ResourceManager service to fetch cluster metrics will be:

```
http://master:8088/ws/v1/cluster/metrics.
```

HTTP request and response

Each URI is associated with HTTP request and response objects. For HTTP requests, currently only the `GET` method is supported. However, newer versions of Hadoop-YARN support more HTTP methods, such as `PUT`, `POST`, and `DELETE`.

A `request` object can have custom headers for accept and accept-encoding headers, and so on. Currently, accept-encoding headers support the `gzip` format and return the compressed output in the same format.

Successful response

YARN services support responses in either JSON or XML format. A successful response will contain the data based on the REST call. The sample successful `response` object will look like the following:

```
{
  "clusterMetrics": {
    "containersPending": 0,
    "allocatedVirtualCores": 0,
```

```
    "lostNodes": 0,
    "totalNodes": 1,
    "activeNodes": 1,
    "containersReserved": 0,
    "appsRunning": 0,
    "availableVirtualCores": 8,
    "appsFailed": 0,
    "availableMB": 8192,
    "allocatedMB": 0,
    "appsSubmitted": 1,
    "appsPending": 0,
    "unhealthyNodes": 0,
    "decommissionedNodes": 0,
    "appsKilled": 0,
    "totalMB": 8192,
    "reservedMB": 0,
    "rebootedNodes": 0,
    "appsCompleted": 1,
    "reservedVirtualCores": 0,
    "totalVirtualCores": 8,
    "containersAllocated": 0
  }
}
```

Response with an error

In the event of an exception or invalid request, the `response` object will contain the exception type, the name of the Java class involved, and the exception message. The following is the sample error response object:

```
{
    "RemoteException" : {
        "javaClassName" :
"org.apache.hadoop.yarn.webapp.NotFoundException",
        "exception" : "NotFoundException",
        "message" : "java.lang.Exception: app with id: <app_id> not
found"
    }
}
```

ResourceManager REST APIs

YARN ResourceManager APIs allow the user or administrator to obtain cluster metrics, lists of NodeManager nodes, scheduler information, associated applications, and so on. As mentioned in the previous chapters, the default port for the ResourceManager web application is `8088`. An administrator can configure the web application address using the `yarn.resourcemanager.webapp.address` property in the `yarn-site.xml` file:

```
<property>
    <name>yarn.resourcemanager.webapp.address</name>
    <value>master:8088</value>
</property>
```

The ResourceManager REST APIs can be grouped as:

- Cluster summary
- Scheduler details
- Nodes
- Applications

The cluster summary

There are two URIs to fetch cluster meta-information such as the deployed version, available memory, cluster capabilities, nodes available, and so on:

- **Cluster metadata**: This API provides overall information about the cluster, including the state and version of ResourceManager and Hadoop:
    - **URI**: `http://<RM Http Address:Port>/ws/v1/cluster/info`
    - **Example**: `http://master:8088/ws/v1/cluster/info`

- **Cluster metrics**: This API provides the overall cluster metrics. It provides total applications submitted to the cluster and the current state of containers, cores, and nodes in the cluster:
    - **URI**: `http://<RM Http Address:Port>/ws/v1/cluster/metrics`
    - **Example**: `http://master:8088/ws/v1/cluster/metrics`

Scheduler details

The scheduler API provides detailed information about the scheduler and the queues configured for the cluster. The response object also provides information on active and pending applications in the cluster and the queues to which the application belongs. The scheduler information in the response object is based on the type of scheduler configured (capacity or fair):

- **URI**: `http://<RM Http Address:Port>/ws/v1/cluster/scheduler`
- **Example**: `http://master:8088/ws/v1/cluster/scheduler`

Nodes

The node APIs provide the details of all nodes (or a specific node) in the cluster. They provide rack information, state, health, cores, and memory information, and so on, for each node:

- **Nodes list**: A list of nodes part of YARN cluster:
    - **URI**: `http://<RM Http Address:Port>/ws/v1/cluster/nodes`
    - **Example**: `http://master:8088/ws/v1/cluster/nodes`

- **Single node information:** Node information for a single node passed as a part of the URI:
    - **URI**: `http://<RM Http Address:Port>/ws/v1/cluster/nodes/{nodeid}`
    - **Example**: `http://master:8088/ws/v1/cluster/nodes/node1:57168`

Applications

Application APIs provide information related to a collection of application objects or a specific application. The application details contain information such as application name, user, state, application type, and so on. You can also use application APIs to fetch information related to application attempts.

- **Applications list**: This API provides the list of all applications associated with the cluster. It also supports a few query parameters to filter the required application list:
    - **URI**: `http://<RM Http Address:Port>/ws/v1/cluster/apps`
    - **Example**: `http://master:8088/ws/v1/cluster/apps`

Following is the supported query parameter list:

Query parameter	Description
states	Applications with the specified state or set of states provided as a comma-separated list, for example RUNNING, FINISHED
finalStatus	Final status of the application matched with specified value
user	Applications submitted by the specified user
queue	Queue information of all applications
limit	Limits the total application information returned
startedTimeBegin	Applications having specified start time of execution (in milliseconds)
startedTimeEnd	Applications with start time ending at a specified time (in milliseconds)
finishedTimeBegin	Applications having specified finish time of execution (in milliseconds)
finishedTimeEnd	Applications with end time equivalent to specified time (in milliseconds)
applicationTypes	Applications with specified application type or a comma-separated list of types
applicationTags	Applications with specified application tag or a comma-separated list of tags

- **Applications statistics**: The statistics API provides the count of different applications executed over the cluster. This API returns a triplet of application type, application state, and number of applications of this type. It supports a few query parameters to filter the statistics based on application state or application type. Currently, one application type at most is supported as a query parameter:
  - **URI**: http://<RM Http Address:Port>/ws/v1/cluster/appstatistics
  - **Example**: http://master:8088/ws/v1/cluster/appstatisatics

Following is the supported query parameter list:

Query parameter	Description
States	Comma-separated list of application states
applicationTypes	Comma-separated list of application types

- **Single application information**: This API provides information about a particular application executed on the cluster. The response includes tracking URL, running containers, status, queue, and other important information about the application:
    - URI: http://<RM Http Address:Port>/ws/v1/cluster/apps/{appid}
    - Example: http://master:8088/ws/v1/cluster/apps/application_142018169_0001
- **Application attempts**: This API provides an object for all the attempts made to execute an application. It includes the container and NodeManager host address of each attempt:
    - URI: http://<RM Http Address:Port>/ws/v1/cluster/apps/{appid}/appattempts
    - Example: http://master:8088/ws/v1/cluster/apps/application_1428169_0001/appattempts

To read more about ResourceManager REST APIs, refer to the Hadoop-YARN documentation at http://hadoop.apache.org/docs/r2.5.1/hadoop-yarn/hadoop-yarn-site/ResourceManagerRest.html.

NodeManager REST APIs

YARN NodeManager APIs allow the user or administrator to obtain the node resource metrics, health status of the node, list of applications and containers associated with that node, and so on. The default port for NodeManager's web application is 8042. An administrator can configure the web application address using the yarn.nodemanager.webapp.address property in the yarn-site.xml file.

NodeManager REST APIs can be grouped as:

- Node summary
- Applications
- Containers

The node summary

This API provides metadata about the node, which includes the version of the NodeManager service, host name, node status, resource utilization, and more:

- **Node metadata**: The summary for the node:
    - **URI**: `http://<NM Http Address:Port>/ws/v1/node/info`
    - **Example**: `http://node1:8042/ws/v1/node/info`

Applications

Similar to the ResourceManager API, the application APIs for NodeManager provide information related to a collection of application objects or a specific application that is associated with the NodeManager.

The metadata of application includes application ID, user name, application state and list of application containers.

- **Applications list**: A list of applications that are associated with a particular node:
    - **URI**: `http://<NM Http Address:Port>/ws/v1/node/apps`
    - **Example**: `http://node1:8042/ws/v1/node/apps`

Following is the supported query parameter list:

Query parameter	Description
state	Comma-separated list of application states
user	Comma-separated list of user names

- **Single application information**: Information of a single application with application ID passed as part of the URI:
    - **URI**: `http://<NM Http Address:Port>/ws/v1/node/apps/{appid}`
    - **Example**: `http://node:8042/ws/v1/node/apps/application_142018169_0001`

Containers

Similar to the application API, the NodeManager service exposes the container API. You can either view all the containers associated to a node or fetch details of a particular container:

- **Containers list**: A list of containers running on a node:
    - ○ **URI**: `http://<NM Http Address:Port>/ws/v1/node/containers`
    - ○ **Example**: `http://node1:8042/ws/v1/node/containers`

- **Single container information**: Information of a container specified as a part of URI:
    - ○ **URI**: `http://<NM Http Address:Port>/ws/v1/node/containers/{containerId}`
    - ○ **Example**: `http://node1:8042/ws/v1/node/containers/container_201434_123`

To read more about NodeManager REST APIs, refer to the Hadoop-YARN documentation at `http://hadoop.apache.org/docs/r2.5.1/hadoop-yarn/hadoop-yarn-site/NodeManagerRest.html`.

MapReduce ApplicationMaster REST APIs

MapReduce ApplicationMaster REST APIs provide information about the running ApplicationMaster service. As mentioned in the earlier chapters, MapReduce ApplicationMaster is an application-specific service that manages execution of MapReduce job over a Hadoop-YARN cluster.

The URI format of MapReduce ApplicationMaster REST services is:

`http://<proxy http address:port>/proxy/{appid}/ws/v1/mapreduce`

MapReduce ApplicationMaster REST APIs are accessed using a proxy server, that is, Web Application Proxy server. Proxy server is an optional service in YARN. An administrator can configure the service to run on a particular host or on the ResourceManager itself (stand-alone mode). If the proxy server is not configured, then it runs as a part of the ResourceManager service.

By default, REST calls could be made to the web address port of ResourceManager `8088`. It could also be explicitly set using the `yarn.web-proxy.address` property in the `yarn-site.xml` file.

To read more about the Web Application proxy server, refer to the Hadoop documentation at `http://hadoop.apache.org/docs/r2.5.1/hadoop-yarn/hadoop-yarn-site/WebApplicationProxy.html`

MapReduce ApplicationMaster REST APIs can be grouped as:

- ApplicationMaster summary
- Jobs
- Tasks

ApplicationMaster summary

This API provides information about ApplicationMaster, including application ID, application name, start time, and time elapsed:

- **ApplicationMaster metadata**: The information for ApplicationMaster service:
  - ○ **URI**: `http://<proxy http address:port>/proxy/{appid}/ws/ v1/mapreduce/info`
  - ○ **Example**: `http://master:8088/proxy/ application_2014554343_0001/ws/v1/mapreduce/info`

Jobs

Job APIs provide information related to the MapReduce jobs associated with ApplicationMaster. As per the current implementation, ApplicationMaster is associated with a single MapReduce job. The APIs are used to access job attempts, counters, and tasks, as explained in the following:

- **Jobs list**: List of jobs associated with the application:
  - ○ **URI**: `http://<proxy http address:port>/proxy/{appid}/ws/ v1/mapreduce/jobs`
  - ○ **Example**: `http://master:8088/proxy/ application_2014554343_0001/ws/v1/mapreduce/jobs`

- **Single job information**: Information of a single job specified as part of the URI:
  - ○ **URI**: `http://<proxy http address:port>/proxy/{appid}/ws/ v1/mapreduce/jobs/{jobid}`
  - ○ **Example**: `http://master:8088/proxy/ application_2014554343_0001/ws/v1/mapreduce/jobs/ job__2014554343_0001`

- **Job attempts**: This API provides a collection of job attempts corresponding to a job. It provides the attempt ID, node ID, HTTP address of the node, link to log files, container ID, and start time of each attempt:

    ○ **URI**: `http://<proxy http address:port>/proxy/{appid}/ws/v1/mapreduce/jobs/{jobid}/jobattempts`

    ○ **Example**: `http://master:8088/proxy/application_2014554343_0001/ws/v1/mapreduce/jobs/job__2014554343_0001/jobattempts`

- **Job counters**: This API provides all counters for a job executed over the YARN cluster. Each counter contains the name, map counter value, reduce counter value, and total counter value. It provides counters for following set of groups:

    `Shuffle errors`

    `FileSystemCounter`

    `TaskCounter`

    `FileInputFormatCounter`

    `FileOutputFormatCounter`

    ○ **URI**: `http://<proxy http address:port>/proxy/{appid}/ws/v1/mapreduce/jobs/{jobid}/counters`

    ○ **Example**: `http://master:8088/proxy/application_2014554343_0001/ws/v1/mapreduce/jobs/job__2014554343_0001/counters`

- **Job configuration**: This API provides configurations for the specified job. It provides the path of the job configuration file `job.xml` and the name, value, and source of all configurations defined for the job. The source specifies the mode by which the property is defined. The valid values are:

    `hdfs-site.xml`

    `job.xml`

    `programmatically`

    `mapred-site.xml`

    ○ **URI**: `http://<proxy http address:port>/proxy/{appid}/ws/v1/mapreduce/jobs/{jobid}/conf`

    ○ **Example**: `http://master:8088/proxy/application_2014554343_0001/ws/v1/mapreduce/jobs/job__2014554343_0001/conf`

Tasks

Similar to the NodeManager jobs API, task APIs provide information related to each MapReduce task associated with a MapReduce job. The APIs are used to fetch the task list, summary, attempts, and attempt counters:

- **Tasks list**: Each task object contains the task ID, current progress, current state, elapsed time, start time, task type, and so on:
  - ○ **URI**: `http://<proxy http address:port>/proxy/{appid}/ws/v1/mapreduce/jobs/{jobid}/tasks`
  - ○ **Example**: `http://master:8088/proxy/application_2014554343_0001/ws/v1/mapreduce/jobs/job_2014554343_0001/tasks`

Following is the supported query parameter list:

Query parameter	Description
type	Valid values are m or z: m for map task and z for reduce task

- **Single task information**: Information of a single task specified as part of the URI:
  - ○ **URI**: `http://<proxy http address:port>/proxy/{appid}/ws/v1/mapreduce/jobs/{jobid}/tasks/{taskid}`
  - ○ **Example**: `http://master:8088/proxy/application_2014554343_0001/ws/v1/mapreduce/jobs/job_2014554343_0001/tasks/task_0001`

- **Task counters**: This API provides the counters of a job's task corresponding to an application. The counter groups are same as that of a job:
  - ○ **URI**: `http://<proxy http address:port>/proxy/{appid}/ws/v1/mapreduce/jobs/{jobid}/tasks/{taskid}/counters`
  - ○ **Example**: `http://master:8088/proxy/application_2014554343_0001/ws/v1/mapreduce/jobs/job_2014554343_0001/tasks/task_0001/counters`

- **Task attempts**: This API provides a collection of attempts corresponding to a task. It provides attempt ID, state, rack, node http address, attempt type, start time, assigned container ID etc. for each attempt:
  - ○ **URI**: `http://<proxy http address:port>/proxy/{appid}/ws/v1/mapreduce/jobs/{jobid}/tasks/{taskid}/attempts`

○ **Example**: `http://master:8088/proxy/`
  `application_2014554343_0001/ws/v1/mapreduce/jobs/`
  `job_2014554343_0001/tasks/task_0001/attempts`

- **Single task attempt information**: Information of a single task attempt specified as part of the URI:

  ○ **URI**: `http://<proxy http address:port>/proxy/{appid}/`
    `ws/v1/mapreduce/jobs/{jobid}/tasks/{taskid}/attempts/`
    `{attempt id}`

  ○ **Example**: `http://master:8088/proxy/`
    `application_2014554343_0001/ws/v1/mapreduce/jobs/`
    `job_2014554343_0001/tasks/task_0001/attempts/`
    `attempt_0001`

- **Task attempt counters**: This API provides the counters of the specified attempt:

  ○ **URI**: `http://<proxy http address:port>/proxy/{appid}/`
    `ws/v1/mapreduce/jobs/{jobid}/tasks/{taskid}/attempts/`
    `{attempt id}/counters`

  ○ **Example**: `http://master:8088/proxy/`
    `application_20145543_0001/ws/v1/mapreduce/jobs/`
    `job_20145543_0001/tasks/task_0001/attempts/attempt_0001/`
    `counters`

To read more about NodeManager REST APIs, refer to the Hadoop-YARN documentation at `http://hadoop.apache.org/docs/r2.5.1/hadoop-mapreduce-client/hadoop-mapreduce-client-core/MapredAppMasterRest.html`.

MapReduce HistoryServer REST APIs

HistorySever maintains information of MapReduce applications executed over the cluster. The Rest API provides counters, attempts, and configuration information about the jobs and tasks. MapReduce HistoryServer starts at web address port `19888` by default. This could be configured by setting up the `mapreduce.jobhistory.webapp.address` property in the `mapred-site.xml` file.

MapReduce HistoryServer REST APIs provide information about the finished applications executed over the cluster. These APIs have similar URI structures and information types as the MapReduce ApplicationMaster API. The MapReduce ApplicationMaster API is used when the application is in RUNNING state. However, once the application is finished, the application data is accessed through the MapReduce HistoryServer API.

The URI format for MapReduce HistoryServer REST services is:

```
http://<history server http address:port>/ws/v1/history
```

> MapReduce Job HistoryServer REST APIs are accessed using a job HistoryServer daemon configured with the MapReduce framework in Hadoop. A cluster administrator needs to configure the service using the `mapreduce.jobhistory.webapp.address` property in the `mapred-site.xml` file.
>
> The default HTTP port for HistoryServer is `19888` and it uses port `10020` as the RPC port for internal communication.

To read more about NodeManager REST APIs, refer to the Hadoop-YARN documentation at `http://hadoop.apache.org/docs/r2.5.1/hadoop-mapreduce-client/hadoop-mapreduce-client-hs/HistoryServerRest.html`.

How to access REST services

The preceding sections in the chapter cover the list of URIs exposed by YARN. In this section, you will learn about three different ways to fetch data from these services:

- REST client plugins
- Curl command
- Java API

RESTClient plugins

You can use plugins available for different web browsers to fetch data from YARN REST services. The `RESTClient` plugin can be used in Firefox. To install or read more about the plugin, refer to `https://addons.mozilla.org/en-us/firefox/addon/restclient/`:

Following are the steps to use RESTClient in Firefox:

1. After successful installation, open the **RESTClient** page in your Firefox browser. The page contains a menu section and a request section:

2. From the menu section, add a **Custom Header** to the request:

3. Enter `Accept` and `application/json` in the **Name** and **Value** fields of the header, respectively. If you need the response as XML data, then specify the value of the `Accept` header as `application/xml`:

4. Specify request URI: In the request section, choose the `request` method and specify the URI for the REST service. In this example, specify the ResourceManager's cluster metrics URI and select the `request` method as GET. A sample URI for cluster metrics is `http://master:8088/ws/v1/cluster/metrics`:

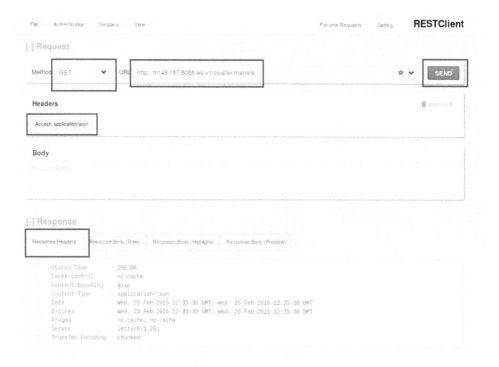

To send your request to the ResourceManager service, click on the **Send** button:

- **View response**: A response section containing the response headers and body is automatically added to the page. The body contains the information in the JSON / XML format based on the request header specified.

- **JSON response**:

```
1.  {
2.      "clusterMetrics":
3.      {
4.          "appsSubmitted": 0,
5.          "appsCompleted": 0,
6.          "appsPending": 0,
7.          "appsRunning": 0,
8.          "appsFailed": 0,
9.          "appsKilled": 0,
10.         "reservedMB": 0,
11.         "availableMB": 16384,
12.         "allocatedMB": 0,
13.         "reservedVirtualCores": 0,
14.         "availableVirtualCores": 16,
15.         "allocatedVirtualCores": 0,
16.         "containersAllocated": 0,
17.         "containersReserved": 0,
18.         "containersPending": 0,
19.         "totalMB": 16384,
20.         "totalVirtualCores": 16,
21.         "totalNodes": 2,
22.         "lostNodes": 0,
23.         "unhealthyNodes": 0,
24.         "decommissionedNodes": 0,
25.         "rebootedNodes": 0,
26.         "activeNodes": 2
27.      }
28.  }
```

- **XML response**:

[-] Response

| Response Headers | Response Body (Raw) | Response Body (Highlight) | Response Body (Preview) |

```
<?xml version="1.0" encoding="UTF-8" standalone="yes"?>
<clusterMetrics>
  <appsSubmitted>0</appsSubmitted>
  <appsCompleted>0</appsCompleted>
  <appsPending>0</appsPending>
  <appsRunning>0</appsRunning>
  <appsFailed>0</appsFailed>
  <appsKilled>0</appsKilled>
  <reservedMB>0</reservedMB>
  <availableMB>16384</availableMB>
  <allocatedMB>0</allocatedMB>
  <reservedVirtualCores>0</reservedVirtualCores>
  <availableVirtualCores>16</availableVirtualCores>
  <allocatedVirtualCores>0</allocatedVirtualCores>
  <containersAllocated>0</containersAllocated>
  <containersReserved>0</containersReserved>
  <containersPending>0</containersPending>
  <totalMB>16384</totalMB>
  <totalVirtualCores>16</totalVirtualCores>
  <totalNodes>2</totalNodes>
  <lostNodes>0</lostNodes>
  <unhealthyNodes>0</unhealthyNodes>
  <decommissionedNodes>0</decommissionedNodes>
  <rebootedNodes>0</rebootedNodes>
  <activeNodes>2</activeNodes>
</clusterMetrics>
```

Curl command

`Curl` is a command-line tool used to transfer data with the URL. It uses the `libcurl` library, a client-side URL library that supports file transfer with multiple protocols, such as FTP, FTPS, HTTP, HTTPS, SFTP, and Telnet. To install and read more about the `curl` command, refer to the official website at `http://curl.haxx.se/`:

- **Calling REST API using curl**: You can use the `curl` command on the Linux as well as Windows system. Following are the basic command options for the `curl` command and information on how you can fetch data from REST services on Linux systems:

- **Syntax**: `curl [options] [URL...]`

- **Command options**:

    -h prints the usage options for `curl` command

    -i shows http response headers

    -H allows you to set http request headers

    -d allows you to set the request body

    -v enable interactive

- **Sample curl command**:

    ```
    curl -v -H "Accept: application/json" -X GET
    http://master:8088/ws/v1/cluster/metrics
    ```

    ```
    curl -v -H "Accept: application/xml" -X GET
    http://master:8088/ws/v1/cluster/metrics
    ```

Java API

A Java developer can fetch REST data using the classes defined in the `java.net` package. Here is a small example that connects to the YARN REST service and retrieves the required JSON/XML data. In this section, we'll walk through an example to write a Java API, create an executable `jar`, and execute to fetch the data in JSON format.

Follow these steps to create and execute a runnable `jar`:

1.   Create a new Java project in Eclipse and name it `YarnRestClient`:

2.   Download `json-simple-1.1.jar` from `http://code.google.com/p/json-simple/` and add it to the build path of the project.

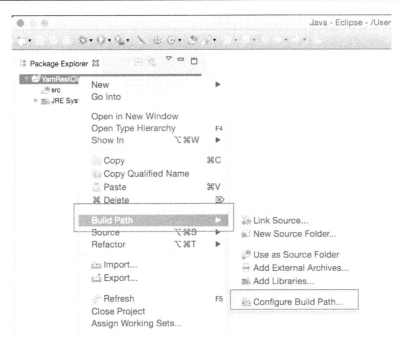

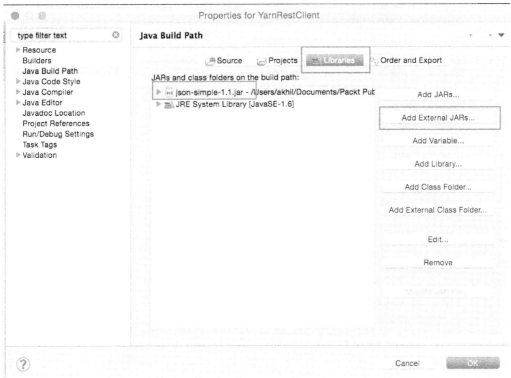

3. Select the `src` directory and create a new Java package with the name `hadoop.yarn.rest.client`:

4. Select the package and create a new class with the name `CallableRequest`, which implements the `java.util.concurrent.Callable` interface. Add the following code to the class:

```
package hadoop.yarn.rest.client;

import java.io.BufferedReader;
import java.io.InputStreamReader;
import java.io.OutputStream;
import java.net.HttpURLConnection;
import java.net.URL;
import java.util.concurrent.Callable;

import org.json.simple.JSONObject;
import org.json.simple.parser.JSONParser;

public class CallableRequest implements Callable<JSONObject> {

    String url;

    public CallableRequest(String url) {
      this.url = url;
    }
```

```
private String getRequest(String urlPath, String input) {
 HttpURLConnection conn = null;
 String output = "";
 OutputStream os = null;
 try {
   URL url = new URL(urlPath);
   conn = (HttpURLConnection) url.openConnection();
   conn.setDoOutput(true);
   conn.setRequestMethod("GET");
   conn.setRequestProperty("Accept", "application/json");
   conn.setRequestProperty("Content-type", "application/json");
   if (input != null && !input.isEmpty()) {
    os = conn.getOutputStream();
    os.write(input.getBytes());
    os.flush();
   }
   String buffer = "";
   BufferedReader br;

   br = new BufferedReader(new InputStreamReader(
       (conn.getInputStream())));

   while ((buffer = br.readLine()) != null) {
    output += buffer;
   }
 } catch (Exception e) {
   return null;
 } finally {
   if (conn != null) {
    conn.disconnect();
   }
   if (os != null) {
    try {
      os.close();
    } catch (Exception e) {
      // TODO: handle exception
    }
   }
 }
 return output;
}
```

```java
@Override
public JSONObject call() throws Exception {
  JSONObject json = null;

  String data = this.getRequest(url, null);

  if (data == null) {
    throw new Exception("Could not fetch data from " + url);
  } else {
    json = (JSONObject) new JSONParser().parse(data);
  }
  return json;
  }
}
```

5. The class contains a `getRequest()` method and overrides the call() method of the `Callable` class. The `getRequest()` method connects to the specified URL and returns the `json` result as `JSONObject` data.

6. Select the package and create a new class with name `SampleClient`, which contains the main method. Add the following code to the class:

```
package hadoop.yarn.rest.client;

import java.util.concurrent.ExecutorService;
import java.util.concurrent.Executors;
import java.util.concurrent.FutureTask;
import java.util.concurrent.TimeUnit;

import org.json.simple.JSONObject;

public class SampleClient {

  public static void main(String[] args) {

    try {
      long waitTime = 10000;
      CallableRequest callableRequest = new
CallableRequest(args[0]);
      FutureTask<JSONObject> getRequestTask = new
FutureTask<JSONObject>(
          callableRequest);

      ExecutorService executor = Executors.newFixedThreadPool(1);
      executor.execute(getRequestTask);

      JSONObject beanObject = getRequestTask.get(waitTime,
          TimeUnit.MILLISECONDS);
      if (beanObject == null) {
       System.out.println("Error: Unable to get JSON response.");
      } else {
       System.out.println("JSON Response:");
       System.out.println(beanObject.toJSONString());
      }
    } catch (Exception e) {
      System.out.println("Exception: " + e.getMessage());
      e.printStackTrace();
```

```
    }
    System.exit(0);
    }
}
```

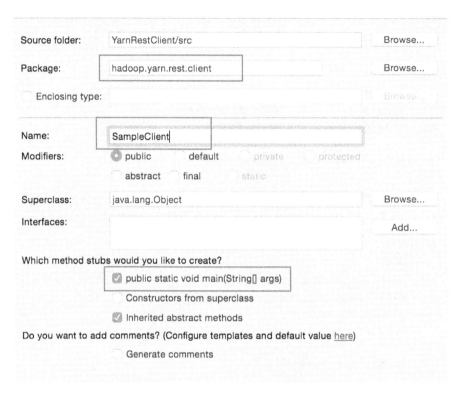

Source folder:	YarnRestClient/src	Browse...
Package:	hadoop.yarn.rest.client	Browse...
☐ Enclosing type:		Browse...

Name:	SampleClient	
Modifiers:	⦿ public ☐ default ☐ private ☐ protected
	☐ abstract ☐ final ☐ static
Superclass:	java.lang.Object	Browse...
Interfaces:		Add...

Which method stubs would you like to create?

☑ public static void main(String[] args)

☐ Constructors from superclass

☑ Inherited abstract methods

Do you want to add comments? (Configure templates and default value here)

☐ Generate comments

7. The main method accepts a URL as the first argument. It connects to the specified URL and prints the result on the console. The package structure appears as in the following screenshot:

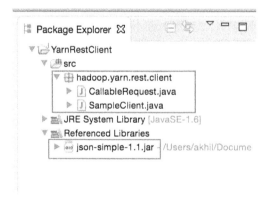

8. In the **Run Configurations** section of the project, add a ResourceManager REST API URL (such as `http://master:8088/ws/v1/cluster/metrics`) as an argument. Ensure that the ResourceManager service is up and running:

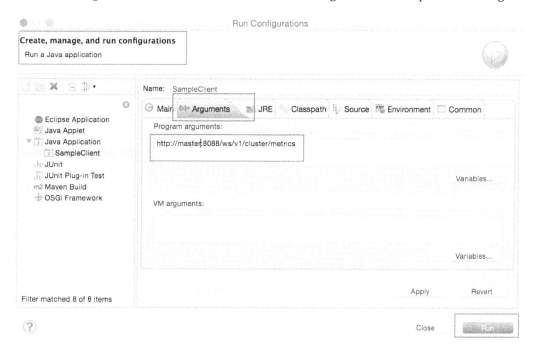

9. Click on **Run** to run the project as a Java application and the output of the program will look like the following:

```
JSON Response:
{"clusterMetrics":{"containersPending":0,"allocatedVirtualC
ores":0,"lostNodes":0,"totalNodes":1,"activeNodes":1,"conta
inersReserved":0,"appsRunning":0,"availableVirtualCores":8,
"appsFailed":0,"availableMB":8192,"allocatedMB":0,"appsSubm
itted":1,"appsPending":0,"unhealthyNodes":0,"decommissioned
Nodes":0,"appsKilled":0,"totalMB":8192,"reservedMB":0,"rebo
otedNodes":0,"appsCompleted":1,"reservedVirtualCores":0,"to
talVirtualCores":8,"containersAllocated":0}}
```

10. You can copy the JSON output and view it using an online JSON editor like `http://jsoneditoronline.org/`.

11. Use the **Runnable Jar File Export** option to export the project and save the `jar` with the name `hadoop-yarn-rest-client.jar`:

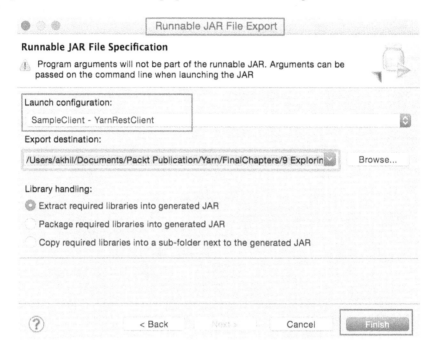

12. Open the terminal and execute the Java command using the `jar` created in the previous step. The output of the command will contain the JSON response of the REST API as follows:

```
java -jar hadoop-yarn-rest-client.jar
http://master:8088/ws/v1/cluster/metrics
```

Use the sample client application to fetch data from YARN REST services.

Summary

YARN services expose a set of URIs as REST APIs to fetch information related to clusters, nodes, applications, jobs, and more. The response format for these REST APIs is configurable as JSON or XML. These APIs provide useful information to monitor cluster resources and application execution. In this chapter, we covered the different REST APIs available in YARN and looked at how we can access them through web browsers and tools such as Curl. This chapter also covered the REST APIs defined for MapReduce ApplicationMaster and JobHistoryServer services. In the next chapter, we'll discuss the different scheduling algorithms defined in YARN and understand how these schedulers can easily be configured with your cluster.

10
Scheduling YARN Applications

In YARN, scheduling means allocation of cluster resources to applications running in the cluster. Scheduler is one of the core components of the ResourceManager service and is responsible for allocation of resources based on the container resource requirements. **Random Access Memory** (**RAM**) and the processor are the two critical resources required for execution of every container. With an increasing number of concurrent containers, fulfilling the resource requirements for each container and resource management for clusters becomes critical for the successful execution of applications.

In this chapter, you will learn about the scheduling mechanisms in YARN and how schedulers can be configured. You will also learn about queues and different scheduling algorithms available in YARN.

We will cover the following topics:

- Introduction to scheduling in YARN
- Introduction to queues and queue types
- Capacity scheduler
- Fair scheduler

An introduction to scheduling in YARN

YARN schedulers are the efficient algorithms written to manage cluster resources. YARN's ResourceManager service has a pluggable and pure scheduler component, that is, it does not monitor or track the applications running in the cluster. It is responsible only for allocation of resources to running applications.

You might be wondering, what is resource allocation and why it is important? Well, let's consider a simple scenario. Suppose an organization has a 100 nodes Hadoop-YARN cluster and there are N teams (for example, A, B, ... N) using the same cluster. Each team has around 10-15 members and each team member can submit YARN applications on the cluster. In order to provide a shared multitenant and efficient cluster utilization, cluster resource allocation plays an important role for a cluster administrator. The cluster resources are divided among the different teams or team members based on a pluggable policy. While defining sharing parameters, the scheduler should be flexible enough to support the following scenarios:

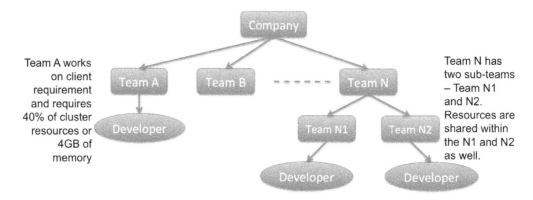

Team A works on client requirement and requires 40% of cluster resources or 4GB of memory

Team N has two sub-teams – Team N1 and N2. Resources are shared within the N1 and N2 as well.

- Suppose **Team A** works on client requirements and all the jobs require 40 percent of the cluster resources. The cluster administrator needs to ensure that the resource requirements for **Team A** are fulfilled as they work for the client.

- A team has multiple subteams and the resources need to be shared among those subteams as well. That is, if a total of 20 percent of cluster resources are allocated to **Team N**, then this 20 percent share is to be distributed among the different subteams as well.

The Hadoop-YARN has two predefined schedulers as follows:

- **Capacity scheduler**: This is a division of resources as a percentage of total cluster resources
- **Fair scheduler**: This is a division of resources based on memory and processor requirements

To configure and use schedulers, an administrator needs to first define queues. Before covering these schedulers in detail, we'll learn about the queues concept and the different type of queues defined in YARN.

An overview of queues

Queues are the data structures or placeholders for the applications submitted to the YARN cluster. A queue is a logical grouping of applications submitted to the YARN cluster. An application is always submitted to a queue. The scheduler then dequeues the applications based on certain parameters to allocate resources and to initiate application execution.

The basic structure of a queue is defined using an interface `org.apache.hadoop.yarn.server.resourcemanager.scheduler.Queue`, as shown in the following diagram:

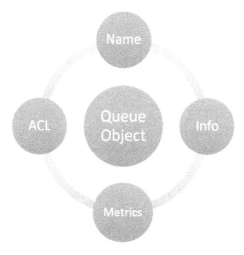

A queue object contains the following information:

- **Queue name**: This is a name assigned to the queue. In case of hierarchical queues, the complete path to the queue is the name along with the parent queue name. We'll discuss about the hierarchical queues in detail later.

- **Queue information**: YARN defines an abstract class `QueueInfo` to store information related to a queue. It is defined in the `org.apache.hadoop.yarn.api.records` package.

  The `QueueInfo` object contains the following information:

    Queue name

    Configured capacity of the queue

    Maximum capacity of the queue

    Current capacity of the queue

    Child queues

    List of running applications

    `QueueState` of the queue

The capacity of a queue is a float value representing the memory assigned to a particular queue. A queue may also contain a list of child queues (hierarchical queues). `RUNNING` and `STOPPED` are two queue states defined in YARN. When a queue is in the `STOPPED` state, it does not accept new application submissions.

- **Queue metrics**: The `QueueMetrics` class is defined in the `org.apache.hadoop.yarn.server.resourcemanager.scheduler` package. It contains statistics for applications, containers and users for a specific queue.

- **Queue Access Control List**: Queue Access Control List is a mechanism to define user and group permissions for a specific queue. You can define a list of users or groups who are allowed to submit applications to the queue. For more details, you can refer to *Chapter 11, Enabling Security in YARN*.

You can view the list of queue objects and their properties either through the ResourceManager web interface or through the ResourceManager REST APIs for scheduler. To read more about the ResourceManager REST APIs, you can refer to the Hadoop documentation at `http://hadoop.apache.org/docs/r2.6.0/hadoop-yarn/hadoop-yarn-site/ResourceManagerRest.html#Cluster_Scheduler_API`.

Types of queues

As mentioned earlier in this chapter, YARN defines two schedulers (capacity and fair schedulers). These schedulers use their own implementation of the queue interface. The following diagram represents a class diagram for different queues defined in YARN:

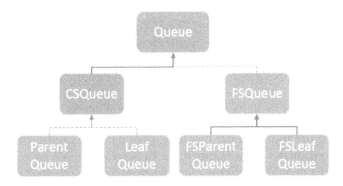

CapacityScheduler Queue (CSQueue)

CSQueue is an interface that extends the Queue interface. It is defined in the org.apache.hadoop.yarn.server.resourcemanager.scheduler.capacity package. The CSQueue interface represents a queue structure for a node in the tree of hierarchical queues for CapacityScheduler.

The two classes that implement the CSQueue interface are as follows:

*   ParentQueue
*   LeafQueue

The properties associated with a CapacityScheduler queue are as follows:

*   yarn.scheduler.capacity.<queue-path>.capacity: This is a float value that specifies the capacity of the queue in percentage (%). At each level of queues (hierarchical queues), the sum of capacities for all queues must be equal to 100. In order to provide elasticity and cluster efficiency, applications may consume more resources than the defined capacity.

*   yarn.scheduler.capacity.<queue-path>.maximum-capacity: It is a float value that specifies the maximum capacity of the queue in percentage (%). This property is used to limit the capacity consumed by the queue. By default, the maximum capacity is set to -1. By default, there's no limit and if cluster resources are available, then the queue can use 100 percent of the resources.

- `yarn.scheduler.capacity.<queue-path>.minimum-user-limit-percent`: This is an integer value that specifies the value that specified the minimum limit in percentage (%) for each user in a queue. When there are multiple users in the same queue, this property enforces the users to get a minimum percentage of cluster resources in a shared environment.

  The default value for the property is 100, that is no user limits are imposed. Suppose, if an administrator has set the value to 20, then if only three users have submitted applications to YARN, then the maximum allowed resources allocated for each user is 33 percent. However, if 5 or more users submit applications, then each user will have a minimum of 20 percent of resources, and if the resources are not available, then the applications will be queued.

- `yarn.scheduler.capacity.<queue-path>.user-limit-factor`: This is a float value that specifies a multiplier value for the queue capacity to allow a user to acquire more cluster resources. For example, if the value is set to 1.5 and the configured queue capacity is 40 percent, then a user in this queue can acquire *60% (1.5 * 40%)* of the cluster resources. The default value is set to 1. It ensures that a user can consume the queue's configured capacity only.

- `yarn.scheduler.capacity.<queue-path>.maximum-applications`: This is an integer value that specifies the maximum count of applications a queue can accept. An application acceptance means applications in running state or queued applications (applications waiting for resource allocation but allocated to a queue). When this limit is reached, the new application submission requests will be rejected.

- `yarn.scheduler.capacity.<queue-path>.maximum-am-resource-percent`: This is a float value that specifies the maximum percent of resources used by ApplicationMaster services.

- `yarn.scheduler.capacity.<queue-path>.state`: This property is used to set the state of the queue. A queue can have either RUNNING or STOPPED state. If a queue is in the STOPPED state, a new application submission requests for a queue or its child queues are rejected.

> You can also refer to the Java code for the interface at
> `http://grepcode.com/file/repo1.maven.org/`
> `maven2/org.apache.hadoop/hadoop-yarn-server-`
> `resourcemanager/2.5.1/org/apache/hadoop/yarn/`
> `server/resourcemanager/scheduler/capacity/`
> `CSQueue.java?av=h#CSQueue`.

FairScheduler Queue (FSQueue)

FSQueue is an abstract class defined in the `org.apache.hadoop.yarn.server.`
`resourcemanager.scheduler.fair` package. It implements the `Queue` interface
and represents the queue's resource computation based on the fair share allocation
of capacity on the basis of total cluster memory.

Similar to `CSQueue`, `FSQueue` represents a queue structure for a node
for `FairScheduler`.

The two classes that extend the `FSQueue` class are as follows:

- `FSParentQueue`
- `FSLeafQueue`

Similar to `CSQueue`, each object of `FSQueue` has the following elements:

- `minResources` and `maxResources`: This is the minimum and maximum
  resources allocated to a queue. The value is in the form `X mb` and `Y vcores`.

- `maxRunningApps`: This is an integer value that specifies the maximum
  number of running or queued applications submitted to a queue.

- `maxAMShare`: This is a float value that specifies the maximum percent of
  resources used by ApplicationMaster services. The default value is `-1.0f` and
  it means that the ApplicationMaster resource usage share check is disabled.

- `weight`: Similar to user limit factor for `CSQueue`, `FSQueue` has a `weight`
  property that specifies a multiplier value for the specified resources to
  allow a user to acquire more resources than other queues.

- `schedulingPolicy`: `FSQueue` uses a scheduling policy for allocating
  resources within a queue. YARN defines three scheduling policies,
  which are as follows:
    - First In First Out policy (FIFO)
    - Fair share policy
    - Dominant Resource Fairness policy (DRF)

  The default policy for a queue is fair. The concept of scheduling policy is
  discussed in detail in the next section.

- `aclSubmitApps` and `aclAdministerApps`: It defines the list of users and
  groups who can submit or kill applications to the queue.

- `minSharePreemptionTimeout`: It is the number of seconds the queue will wait before it will try to acquire containers to use resources from other queues.

 You can also refer to the Java code for the interface at `http://grepcode.com/file/repo1.maven.org/maven2/org.apache.hadoop/hadoop-yarn-server-resourcemanager/2.5.1/org/apache/hadoop/yarn/server/resourcemanager/scheduler/fair/FSQueue.java?av=h#FSQueue`.

An introduction to schedulers

The scheduler is responsible for providing resources to different tasks of running applications. It is only responsible for scheduling of tasks and is not concerned with status tracking and monitoring of tasks. The scheduler ensures meeting resource requirements in terms of memory, cores, disk, and network for the application. At granular level, it meets the resource requirement of containers running for the particular application. The default scheduler of Hadoop uses a single queue (root queue) to accept and schedule applications. It means that all the applications are submitted to the root queue.

You can view the details of the configured scheduler through ResourceManager web UI at `http://<ResourceManager IP>:8088/cluster/scheduler`. This is shown in the following screenshot:

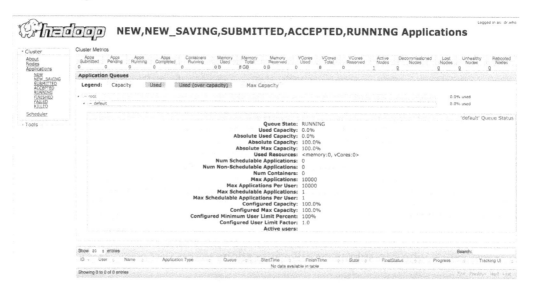

YARN provides interfaces for implementation of pluggable scheduler. The two popular schedulers available with Hadoop are:

- Fair scheduler
- Capacity scheduler

Fair scheduler

Fair scheduler is developed to assign a fair share of resources to all the applications running on the Hadoop YARN cluster. Memory and CPU are the resources currently being distributed fairly among the applications. When a single application is submitted to the cluster, all resources are available to it. When another application is submitted, a part of resources is given to the second application as demanded. Unlike the Hadoop default scheduler, fair scheduler allows parallel execution of short-lived, compute-intensive, and lengthy applications together so that all applications executed in fair time.

A fair scheduler accepts the applications and puts it in a queue. By default, all applications go into a single queue named *default*. Applications could be scheduled to different queues based on the users submitting the application. A scheduling policy is designed for each queue that governs the sharing of resources in the queue.

The applications could be submitted with priorities and queues take care of application priority while scheduling it on cluster. A priority can be set as an integer value while submitting an application. To read more about priority, you can refer to the class `org.apache.hadoop.yarn.api.records.Priority`. In the current version of Hadoop (2.6.0), per application priorities are not passed to the YARN scheduler and default priority for all the applications is set to `1`. You can refer to the `getPriority` method of the `FSAppAttempt` class.

A fair scheduler also guarantees minimum shares to the queues, which means the user or group submitting application to the queue would get the minimum share of resources defined for that queue. When a part of the resources are not utilized by the queue, it will be given to another applications. A fair scheduler also restricts the number of applications executing concurrently on the cluster on per user or per queue basis, though it could accept and queue any number of applications by the user.

In this section, we'll discuss about fair scheduler features and concepts.

Hierarchical queues

A fair scheduler provides support for hierarchical queue. The parent of all user-defined queues is the *root* queue. A root queue can contain any number of children to any level. The queues at the bottom of tree are called as leaf queues.

> Applications are always scheduled through leaf queues. If a user tries to submit an application to a nonleaf queue, then the following exception is returned:
>
> `java.io.IOException: Failed to run job : <Queue_ Name>` is not a leaf queue.

A queue name starts with the parents' queue name followed by the *dot character* and the current queue name. For example, if the *sales* queue is the child of *root*, then the queue path for *sales* will be `root.sales`. Similarly, if *sales* have further children, then their names would be `root.sales.child1` and `root.sales.child2`.

Schedulable

A schedulable is an entity that can initiate a task to run on the cluster. It could be a `Job` or a `Queue`. In YARN, it is an abstract class that could be used to define the algorithms as a fair share that could be applied within a queue or among queues.

Schedulable is of two types — `JobSchedulables` and `QueueSchedulabels`

A schedulable is responsible for the following tasks:

- It can launch tasks through its `assignTask()` interface
- It provides information about the job/queue to the scheduler, including:
    - Demand (the maximum number of tasks required)
    - Number of currently running tasks
    - Minimum share (for queues)
    - Job/queue weight (for fair sharing)
    - Start time and priority (for FIFO)

- It can be assigned a fair share to use with fair scheduling

Scheduling policy

FSQueue uses a scheduling policy for allocating resources within a queue. YARN defines three scheduling policies:

- First In First Out policy (FIFO)
- Fair share policy
- Dominant Resource Fairness policy (DRF)

The FIFO policy is simple and easy to implement. It states that the applications submitted first will get more priority.

The fair share policy is the default scheduling policy for FSQueue. There are three rules for sharing resources fairly:

- Schedulables below their min share of resources are given priority over the schedulables whose minimum share has been met.
- Schedulables below their min share are compared by how far below it they are in terms of ratio. For example, a job A is executed 15 out of minimum share of 20 tasks while another job, B, runs 20 out of minimum share of 40 tasks, then job B is scheduled next because job B is at 50 percent of its min share completion while job A has completed 75 percent of its min share.
- Schedulables above their min share are compared by (running tasks / weight). If all weights are equal, slots are given to the job with the fewest tasks; otherwise, jobs with more weight get proportionally more slots.

A customized policy could be defined by extending the org.apache.hadoop. yarn.server.resourcemanager.scheduler.fair.SchedulingPolicy class. Each queue could be assigned with a different scheduling policy by specifying the schedulingPolicy property for that queue.

> To read more about the fair scheduler, you can refer to the YARN documentation at http://hadoop.apache.org/docs/r2.5.1/ hadoop-yarn/hadoop-yarn-site/FairScheduler.html.

Configuring a fair scheduler

In this section, we'll discuss about the configurations required to set up a fair scheduler. The implementation of a fair scheduler in YARN is defined in the org.apache.hadoop.yarn.server.resourcemanager.scheduler.fair. FairScheduler class. To configure ResourceManager to use fair scheduler, you need to specify the class name in the yarn-site.xml file using property:

```
<property>
<name>yarn.resourcemanager.scheduler.class</name>
<value>org.apache.hadoop.yarn.server.resourcemanager.scheduler.fai
r.FairScheduler</value>
</property>
```

You can also configure the following FairScheduler parameters in the yarn-site.xml file:

Property	Description
yarn.scheduler.fair. allocation.file	A path to an XML file that contains FSQueues definition and their properties.
yarn.scheduler.fair.user-as-default-queue	Use username as the default queue name, if the queue name is not specified.
yarn.scheduler.fair. preemption	Set this to true if pre-emption needs to be enabled.
yarn.scheduler.fair. preemption.cluster-utilization-threshold	This is the resource utilization threshold for pre-emption. The default is 0.8f.
yarn.scheduler.fair. sizebasedweight	This is the weighted share or equal share to all apps irrespective of its size.
yarn.scheduler.fair. update-interval-ms	It is the time interval in milliseconds to calculate a fair share, resource demand, and pre-emption requests. The default value is 500 ms.

Other than the configurations in the yarn-site.xml file, you need to define an allocations file. The allocations file is an .xml file that contains a FSQueues definition and their properties. A sample allocations file for FairScheduler is shown in the following:

```
<?xml version="1.0"?>
<allocations>
  <queue name="queue1" type="parent">
    <minResources>100 mb,1 vcores</minResources>
    <maxResources>8000 mb,8 vcores</maxResources>
    <maxRunningApps>50</maxRunningApps>
```

```
    <queue name="sub_queue1">
      <minResources>100 mb,1 vcores</minResources>
    </queue>
  </queue>

  <queue name="queue2">
    <minResources>1000 mb,1 vcores</minResources>
    <maxResources>6000 mb,5 vcores</maxResources>
    <maxRunningApps>40</maxRunningApps>
    <maxAMShare>0.2</maxAMShare>
    <schedulingPolicy>fifo</schedulingPolicy>
    <weight>1.5</weight>
    <schedulingPolicy>fair</schedulingPolicy>
  </queue>
  <queueMaxAMShareDefault>1.0</queueMaxAMShareDefault>
  <userMaxAppsDefault>5</userMaxAppsDefault>
</allocations>
```

You can save the file as `fair-scheduler.xml` in the configuration folder for Hadoop. You need to specify the file path in the `yarn-site.xml` file using the `property` template:

```
<property>
<name>yarn.scheduler.fair.allocation.file</name>
<value>/home/hduser/hadoop-2.5.1/etc/Hadoop/fair-scheduler.xml</value>
</property>
```

The file may also contain the following properties related to `FairScheduler`:

- `UserElements`
- `userMaxAppsDefault`
- `fairSharePreemptionTimeout`
- `defaultMinSharePreemptionTimeout`
- `queueMaxAppsDefault`
- `queueMaxAMShareDefault`
- `defaultQueueSchedulingPolicy`
- `queuePlacementPolicy`

 To read a detailed explanation about configuration parameters and allocations file, you can refer to the `FairScheduler` documentation at `http://hadoop.apache.org/docs/r2.5.1/hadoop-yarn/hadoop-yarn-site/FairScheduler.html#Configuration`.

After configuring the `yarn-site.xml` file and allocation files, you will need to restart the ResourceManager service. To submit a job to a queue, you need to specify the queue name while submitting the job using `–D` parameters. A sample command to submit the job to `sub_queue1` is shown in the following:

```
yarn jar share/hadoop/mapreduce/hadoop-mapreduce-examples-2.5.1.jar
pi -Dmapreduce.job.queuename=root.queue1.sub_queue1 2 5
```

To view the queue stats, you can refer to the scheduler page through ResourceManager web UI at `http://<ResourceManagerIP>:8088/cluster/scheduler?openQueues=root.queue1#root.queue1.sub_queue1`.

The following screenshot refers to the queue stats for `root.queue1.sub_queue1`:

CapacityScheduler

`CapacityScheduler` is another pluggable scheduler provided by YARN. It allows the execution of multiple applications sharing cluster resources and maximizing throughput of the cluster. It also provides support for multi-tenancy and capacity guarantees. The `CapacityScheduler` uses `CSQueue` objects for queue definition. The implementation of `CapacityScheduler` is defined in the `org.apache.hadoop.yarn.server.resourcemanager.scheduler.capacity.CapacityScheduler` class.

The `CapacityScheduler` offers the following features:

- Hierarchical queues
- Capacity guarantees
- Security

- Elasticity

- Multi-tenancy

- Runtime configuration

- Drain applications

- Resource-based scheduling

To read more about these features, you can refer to the Hadoop documentation at `http://hadoop.apache.org/docs/r2.6.0/hadoop-yarn/hadoop-yarn-site/CapacityScheduler.html`.

Configuring CapacityScheduler

Configuring `CapacityScheduler` in YARN is as simple as configuring `FairScheduler`. To enable `CapacityScheduler`, you need to configure the following property in `yarn-site.xml`:

```
<property>
<name>yarn.resourcemanager.scheduler.class</name>
<value>org.apache.hadoop.yarn.server.resourcemanager.scheduler.cap
acity.CapacityScheduler</value>
</property>
```

Similar to `FairScheduler`, `CapacityScheduler` also has an allocations file. It is an `.xml` file but with a different format than fair scheduler's allocations file. The default allocations file `CapacityScheduler` is `$HADOOP_PREFIX/etc/hadoop/capacity-scheduler.xml`.

The parent queue in `CapacityScheduler` is called root. All user-defined queues will be children of the root queue.

The following `xml` properties defines three queues for `CapacityScheduler` — alpha, beta and default. The queue alpha has two child queues — `a1` and `a2`. At each level, the sum of all the capacities within a queue should be 100 percent.

You can refer to the following capacity scheduler configurations. You might notice that the sum of capacities of child queues of root (`alpha-50`, `beta-30`, and `default-20`) and alpha (`a1-60` and `a2-40`) is 100, as given in the following code:

```
<property>
    <name>yarn.scheduler.capacity.root.queues</name>
    <value>alpha,beta,default</value>
</property>
```

```
<property>
    <name>yarn.scheduler.capacity.root.alpha.capacity</name>
    <value>50</value>
</property>
<property>
    <name>yarn.scheduler.capacity.root.alpha.queues</name>
    <value>a1,a2</value>
</property>
<property>
    <name>yarn.scheduler.capacity.root.alpha.a1.capacity</name>
    <value>60</value>
</property>
<property>
    <name>yarn.scheduler.capacity.root.alpha.a2.capacity</name>
    <value>40</value>
</property>

<property>
    <name>yarn.scheduler.capacity.root.beta.capacity</name>
    <value>30</value>
</property>

<property>
    <name>yarn.scheduler.capacity.root.default.capacity</name>
    <value>20</value>
</property>
```

Similar to `FairScheduler`, to submit a job to a particular queue, you need to specify the queue name using the -D parameter as follows:

```
yarn jar share/hadoop/mapreduce/hadoop-mapreduce-examples-2.5.1.jar pi
-Dmapreduce.job.queuename=a1 5 10
```

The following screenshot shows the stats for queue the `root.alpha.a1` queue during application execution:

Summary

Scheduling in YARN is a pluggable framework to allocate cluster resources in a multiuser environment. In this chapter, you learned about different queues that are defined in YARN. The concepts and parameters related `FSQueue` and `CSQueue`. You also learned about the fair and capacity schedulers that are available in YARN. You also covered an overview about the queue definitions, configurations and job submission for both the schedulers.

In the next chapter, you will learn about the security framework of YARN. You will learn how Kerberos provides an authentication mechanism to YARN and how you can use access control lists.

11
Enabling Security in YARN

A lot of enterprises today use Hadoop and other big data technologies in a production environment. A secured environment has always been a concern for the Hadoop community. A secured environment ensures rightful access to objects in a shared mode by different entities. The objects refer to the data stored in HDFS or local filesystem, applications running on the cluster, and so on. An entity refers to the services within the cluster, clients accessing the cluster, and so on. YARN needs to ensure that the data and logs stored on the local, as well as on the Hadoop filesystem are secured, so that, only authenticated and authorized users can access the information. YARN also exposes data through web applications and REST calls. A perimeter level security should be added in order to secure these applications and calls.

In this chapter, we will cover the following topics:

* Adding security to a YARN cluster
* Working with **Access Control Lists** (**ACLs**)
* An overview of Apache Ranger and Knox

Adding security to a YARN cluster

Hadoop provides a few methods that add security layers to a cluster. YARN inherits those methods and enables security for YARN services.

The following are the methods a cluster administrator can implement while configuring a secure Hadoop-YARN cluster:

Adding Security to YARN	Use dedicated User-Group for Hadoop-YARN daemons
	Validate permissions to YARN directories
	Enable HTTPS protocol
	Enable authorization using Access Control Lists
	Enable authentication using Kerberos

Using a dedicated user group for Hadoop-YARN daemons

Before starting the Hadoop-YARN services, an administrator needs to ensure that a dedicated user group is created on all the nodes of the cluster and all Hadoop-YARN daemons run as the dedicated user only. Hadoop-dedicated users—hdfs, yarn, and mapred must be created on all the nodes and these must belong to a common user group called hadoop.

All the Hadoop-YARN daemons, the ResourceManager, NodeManager, and the Application Timeline server should run under the YARN user. The MapReduce JobHistoryServer service should run as a mapred user.

To create a new group and add new users to the group in Linux, you need to execute the following commands:

- Create a new group:

```
sudo group add <GroupName>
```

- Create a new user for a group:

```
sudo user add -G <GroupName> -p <Password><NewUser>
```

- Sample commands:

```
sudo groupadd hadoop
sudo useradd -G hadoop -p hadoop yarn
```

 You must have root credentials or sudo (admin) access for all the nodes.

Validating permissions to YARN directories

YARN daemons access directories in the HDFS as well as the local filesystem of the node. An administrator needs to ensure that only a dedicated user is set as the owner for the directory and valid permissions are set on these directories.

A list of such directories with their permission details is given here:

Owner (User:Group)	Configuration property	File system	Permissions
yarn:hadoop	`$YARN_LOG_DIR`	Local	drwxrwxr-x
	`yarn.nodemanager.local-dirs`		drwxr-xr-x
	`yarn.nodemanager.log-dirs`		drwxr-xr-x
	`yarn.nodemanager.remote-app-log-dir`	HDFS	drwxrwxrwxt
mapred:hadoop	`mapreduce.jobhistory.intermediate-done-dir`		drwxrwxrwxt
	`mapreduce.jobhistory.done-dir`		drwxr-x---

You can execute the following commands to change the owner of a directory and modify its permissions:

```
chown -R <UserName>:<GroupName> <DirPath>
chmod -R <Octal Code> <DirPath>
```

If there's a permission denied error, then you can use the sudo option for both the commands. The sample commands are as follows:

```
chown -R hdfs:hadoop /home/hduser/hadoop-2.5.1/data/name
chmod -R 700 /home/hduser/hadoop-2.5.1/data/name
```

To read more about the octal code for directory / file permissions, you can refer to the wikipedia page at http://en.wikipedia.org/wiki/File_system_permissions#Numeric_notation.

Enabling the HTTPS protocol

By default, YARN web applications for ResourceManager and TimeLine server use the HTTP protocol. For a secured cluster, a cluster administrator needs to enable the HTTPS protocol by specifying the following property in the `yarn-site.xml` file:

```
<property>
    <name>yarn.http.policy</name>
    <value>HTTPS_ONLY</value>
<property>
```

By default, the value of the above property is set to `HTTP_ONLY`, which uses the HTTP protocol and disables the HTTPS protocol.

An administrator also needs to configure the HTTPS addresses for the YARN daemons by specifying the following properties in the `yarn-site.xml` file:

```
<property>
    <name>yarn.resourcemanager.webapp.https.address</name>
    <value>${yarn.resourcemanager.hostname}:8090</value>
<property>

<property>
    <name>yarn.timeline-service.webapp.https.address</name>
    <value>${yarn.timeline-service.hostname}:8190</value>
<property>
```

The default HTTPS ports for ResourceManager and the TimeLine server daemons are `8090` and `8190`, respectively.

Enabling authorization using Access Control Lists

Access Control Lists are the list of permissions associated with an object in the system. An object can refer to a YARN service, a queue, or an application, and so on. These ACLs are defined as users / groups that are allowed to access or modify an object.

In a Hadoop-YARN cluster, the ACLs check is disabled, by default. You need to configure the `yarn.acl.enable` property in the `yarn-site.xml` file to enable the ACLs:

```
<property>
    <name>yarn.acl.enable</name>
    <value>true</value>
<property>
```

To read more about the ACLs, you can refer to the next section in this chapter, *Working with ACLs*.

Enabling authentication using Kerberos

Kerberos is an authentication protocol used to authenticate the identity of the services running and communicating on different nodes over a nonsecure network. It uses a secret key cryptography mechanism to provide secure authentication. By default, Kerberos authentication is disabled in a Hadoop-YARN cluster. To enable Kerberos authentication in Hadoop, an administrator needs to configure following properties in the `core-site.xml` file:

```
<property>
    <name>hadoop.security.authentication</name>
    <value>kerberos</value>
</property>
<property>
    <name>hadoop.security.authorization</name>
    <value>true</value>
</property>
```

The default value of the `hadoop.security.authentication` property is *simple* that disables Kerberos secure authentication for a cluster. This chapter does not focus on the architecture of Kerberos and its components; instead, this book gives an overview of Hadoop-Kerberos and the basic configuration settings to configure Kerberos with YARN.

The following are the three main Kerberos entities that Hadoop-YARN uses to enable security:

- `realm` – A Kerberos `realm`; in most cases, this is the domain name specified in upper case letters.

- `principal` – A `principal` is a unique identity represented as `username/fully.qualified.domain.name@YOUR-REALM.COM`.

- `keytab` – A `keytab` contains pairs of these principals and encrypted keys (similar to passwords) to authenticate the **key distribution center** (**KDC**).

In a Hadoop-YARN cluster, each daemon is associated with a Kerberos principal name and a keytab file. A cluster administrator needs to configure the principal name and location of the keytab file for each service in the `yarn-site.xml` configuration file.

The following are the properties used for configuring Kerberos:

- `yarn.<service>.keytab`
- `yarn.<service>.principal`

Replace `<service>` with `resourcemanager` and `nodemanager`.

> To read about configuring Kerberos in detail, you can refer to the blogs at
>
> `http://queryio.com/hadoop-big-data-docs/hadoop-big-data-admin-guide/queryio/hadoop-security-setup-kerberos.html` or `http://beadooper.com/?p=206`.

Working with ACLs

In the previous section, we covered a basic overview of ACLs and how to enable ACLs in a Hadoop-YARN cluster. In this section, we'll discuss in depth the implementation of ACLs and the different types of ACLs available for YARN.

Defining an ACL value

ACLs define the authorization rules for an object in a YARN. A cluster administrator can specify a list of users and groups authorized to access the object. It is a comma-separated list of both users and groups. These two lists (users and groups) are separated by a space:

- `user1,user2,user3 group1`: The above ACL value specifies that `user1`, `user2`, `user3` and other users belonging to `group1` are authorized to access the object
- `user1,user2`: If you want to authorize only a specific list of users and do not want any group to access the object, then you can define a list of users with a space at the end
- `group1,group2`: Similarly, if you wish to authorize a list of users belonging to specified groups and no other user to access the object, then you can define a list of groups after a space
- `*`: A special value of `*` implies that there's no restriction and all users are authorized to access the object
- `  `: A special value of blank space implies that no user is authorized to access the object

If an ACL for an object is not defined, then the value of `security.service.authorization.default.acl` is applied.

If `security.service.authorization.default.acl` is not defined, then * is applied.

Type of ACLs

When we work in a multi-user environment, authorization for services, applications, queues is an important concern. Consider the following scenarios in order to understand the need for authorization in a cluster:

- An anonymous user is allowed to submit new applications to the cluster
- A user submits an application and another user kills the application without any notification
- A user that does not belong to a queue is allowed to submit an application to that queue
- A user is able to execute admin commands such as refresh nodes or High Availability, and so on

YARN provides the following four types of ACLs mechanisms to add authorization for objects in a cluster:

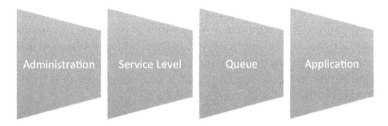

Administration Service Level Queue Application

The administration ACL

A cluster administrator can define a list of users and groups who could be the admin of the YARN cluster. An administrator here refers to a user who can execute the `rmadmin` command for a YARN cluster. To read more about the `rmadmin` command, you can refer to the YARN commands section in *Chapter 3, Administering a Hadoop-YARN Cluster*.

You can add the following property in the `yarn-site.xml` file:

```
<property>
    <name>yarn.admin.acl</name>
    <value>user1,user2 group1</value>
</property>
```

Zookeeper ACLs

YARN supports the feature of state store and high availability for ResourceManager. A cluster administrator can define the following ACL properties for Zookeeper and root `znode` in the `yarn-site.xml` file:

`yarn.resourcemanager.zk-acl`

`yarn.resourcemanager.zk-state-store.root-node.acl`

`yarn.resourcemanager.zk-auth`

To read more about Zookeeper ACLs, you can refer to the Zookeeper documentation at `http://zookeeper.apache.org/doc/trunk/zookeeperProgrammers.html#sc_ZooKeeperAccessControl`.

The service-level ACL

YARN consists of the ResourceManager and NodeManager services running across the cluster. YARN clients connect to these services to execute the applications or to get the cluster status and metrics. Hadoop provides an initial authorization mechanism to ensure the authorization of its services. YARN inherits the same mechanism to provide client service authorization. The service level authorization in Hadoop is defined through a `hadoop.policy.xml` file. The `hadoop.policy.xml` file is located inside the Hadoop configuration directory `HADOOP_CONF_DIR`. The following is the list of ACLs that can be configured through the `hadoop-policy.xml` file:

- `security.resourcetracker.protocol.acl`: This is the ACL for `ResourceTracker` protocol, that is communication between the ResourceManager and NodeManager services

- `security.resourcemanager-administration.protocol.acl`: This is the ACL for `ResourceManagerAdministration` protocol, list of users / groups authorized to execute admin commands

- `security.applicationclient.protocol.acl`: This is the ACL for `ApplicationClient` protocol, that is, communication between the ResourceManager and YARN clients

- `security.applicationmaster.protocol.acl`: This is the ACL for `ApplicationMaster` protocol, that is, communication between the ResourceManager and ApplicationMasters services

- `security.containermanagement.protocol.acl`: This is the ACL for `ContainerManagement` protocol, that is, communication between the NodeManager and ApplicationMasters services

- `security.resourcelocalizer.protocol.acl`: This is the ACL for the `ResourceLocalizer` protocol, that is, communication between the NodeManager and ResourceLocalizer services

For a secured environment, YARN also provides authentication for inter-process communications through SecretManager and tokens. The SecretManager service governs the communication and coordination between different YARN services. The YARN services such as ResourceManager and NodeManager communicate with each other for containers execution, liveliness check, resource localization, and so on. For each communication, it is important to validate the authenticity of the service requesting an information or task execution.

The following implementations of SecretManager are defined in YARN:

- `BaseNMTokenSecretManager`: The NodeManager keys are generated using `NMTokenIdentifier`, which accepts the application attempt ID, node ID, application submitter, and the master key as the input. A unique master key is generated using the `javax.crypto.SecretKey` and `javax.crypto.KeyGenerator` interfaces of the **Java Cryptography Extension (JCE)** APIs.

- `AMRMTokenSecretManager`: AM-RM tokens are generated per application attempt. A secret token is generated and associated with each application attempt. The token is used by the attempt in all further communication. ResourceManager stores information of the tokens in the memory until the application lasts; it is being used for attempt authentication and restart, in case of a failed attempt.

- `BaseClientToAMTokenSecretManager`: This is used to generate tokens for communication between clients, ResourceManager, and the ApplicationMaster services. It has the following two concrete implementations:

  - `ClientToAMTokenSecretManager`: AM validates client-RM tokens issued by ResourceManager to clients. Each AM has only one associated master key.

  - `ClientToAMTokenSecretManagerInRM`: ResourceManager maintains an in-memory list of per application attempt master keys for managing client tokens.

- `BaseContainerTokenSecretManager`: This is used for generating authentication keys for each container. ResourceManager persist the MasterKey in memory and NodeManagers request it from ResourceManager and validate against the container token.

The queue ACL

YARN supports two schedulers—capacity and fair. Both these schedulers manage application scheduling with the help of queues. If the YARN authorization check is enabled, then `QueueACLManager` checks the authorization for each user against the ACLs defined for a queue. Both these schedulers support hierarchical queues that is, parent and leaf queues. An ACL specified for a parent queue will be automatically applied to all of its descendant queues.

For each queue, an administrator can define two authorization checks:

- **Application submission**: A list of users/groups who can submit applications to the given queue.

- **Administer queue**: A list of users/groups who can administer applications on the given queue. Queue administration includes application submission, operations such as viewing or killing an application that is associated with a particular queue.

To specify a queue ACL for the capacity and fair schedulers, you can configure the following queue properties in their respective `.xml` files:

Capacity scheduler	`yarn.scheduler.capacity.root.<queue-path>.acl_submit_applications`
	
	`yarn.scheduler.capacity.root.<queue-path>.acl_administer_queue`

Fair scheduler	`aclSubmitApps`
	
	`aclAdministerApps`

The application ACL

YARN allows users to set ACL for applications. A user can specify the list of users who can view or modify the application. `ApplicationACLsManager` is responsible for authorizing the user's access control to applications running on the Hadoop-YARN cluster. `ApplicationACLsManager` maintains a context of `ApplicationAccessType` and `AccessControlList` for each application scheduled on YARN cluster. The enumeration for `ApplicationAccessType` is defined in the package `org.apache.hadoop.yarn.api.records` with values for `ApplicationAccessType`:

- `VIEW_APP`: This access type specifies who all can view all or some parts of the application's details
- `MODIFY_APP`: This access type specifies who can modify the running application, for example, killing the application

If the YARN authorization check is enabled, `ApplicationACLsManager` checks whether the user is the owner of the application or is authorized to access the application as specified in `ApplicationAccessType`.

To enable and add ACLs for a MapReduce application, you can specify the following properties in the `mapred-site.xml` file inside the configuration folder of Hadoop:

- `mapreduce.cluster.acls.enabled`
- `mapreduce.job.acl-modify-job`
- `mapreduce.job.acl-view-job`

You can also refer to the `mapred-default.xml` file at `http://hadoop.apache.org/docs/r2.5.1/hadoop-mapreduce-client/hadoop-mapreduce-client-core/mapred-default.xml`.

To enable ACLs for a custom application, you will need to define ACLs in `ContainerLaunchContext` for the `AppMaster` container. The sample code to define ACLs is given here:

```
Map<ApplicationAccessType, String>appAclDefinition = new
HashMap<ApplicationAccessType, String>();
appAclDefinition.put(ApplicationAccessType.MODIFY_APP, "*");
appAclDefinition.put(ApplicationAccessType.VIEW_APP, "*");

// amContainer is an instance of ContainerLaunchContext (AppMaster
container definintion in ApplicationSubmissionContext)
amContainer.setApplicationACLs(appAclDefinition);
```

For more information, you can refer to the JAVA API for ContainerLaunchContext at `http://hadoop.apache.org/docs/r2.5.1/api/org/apache/hadoop/yarn/api/records/ContainerLaunchContext.html`.

Other security frameworks

Other than the mentioned security mechanisms, a few security frameworks are being developed. These frameworks are being developed to simplify the security configurations for a cluster administrator. This section will cover a basic overview of the Apache Ranger and Knox projects.

Apache Ranger

Apache Ranger is an incubator project that provides a framework for central management of the Hadoop security policies. It provides a central UI and REST APIs to manage security policies for the Hadoop cluster.

This consists of three components:

- Policy manager
- Plugins
- User group sync

The current release (0.4) supports security administration for the following technologies/frameworks—Hadoop HDFS, Hive, HBase, Storm, and Knox. The next release (0.5) is focused to support authorization and auditing for YARN services. It'll provide support for managing and auditing ACLs for YARN queues.

To read more about Apache Ranger, you can refer to the official website at `http://ranger.incubator.apache.org/`. You can also refer to the Hortonworks documentation at `http://hortonworks.com/hadoop/ranger/`.

Apache Knox

With the introduction of the YARN framework as a generic ResourceManager, integration and adoption of big data technologies and new frameworks is easy. Before adopting any new framework/application, an enterprise needs to maintain compliance with its security policies. Apache Knox is a stateless reverse proxy framework that ensures security compliance adherence and provides perimeter security to a Hadoop cluster. Perimeter security means securing the HTTP/REST based services and providing a proxy gateway between cluster resources and users accessing the cluster. Knox also encapsulates Kerberos and eliminates the need to client side libraries and configuration while accessing a secured Hadoop cluster.

To read more about Apache Knox, you can refer to the official website at http://knox.apache.org/.

You can also refer to the Hortonworks documentation at http://hortonworks.com/hadoop/knox/.

Summary

YARN extends security features available in Hadoop and allows enterprises to secure their production clusters. Security for YARN includes the authentication and authorization of services, directories, applications, queues, and so on. In this chapter, you learned about the methods to enable security in a Hadoop-YARN cluster and had an overview of Kerberos with YARN. This chapter also explained usage of ACLs and overview of Hadoop security projects such as Apache Ranger and Knox. In the next chapter, you will learn about the integration of YARN with other big data technologies such as Spark, Storm, and so on.

12
Real-time Data Analytics Using YARN

Hadoop is known for batch processing of data available in HDFS through MapReduce programming. The data is placed in HDFS before it can be queried for analysis. The Hadoop services execute only MapReduce jobs. The cluster resources are not fully utilized for other operations when the resources are ideal.

This is considered as a limitation for use cases that required processing of data in real time. Apache Storm and Spark are the frameworks developed for processing data in real time. These frameworks need an efficient cluster's ResourceManager. Focusing on a common solution for the preceding limitations in Hadoop, YARN evolved as a generic framework to provide resource management and application execution over a cluster. It not only allows different frameworks other than MapReduce to use the same cluster but also provides efficient scheduling algorithms to the applications running on the cluster. Frameworks such as Storm, Spark, and Giraph adopted YARN for application execution and management.

In this chapter, we will cover the integration of the following technologies with YARN:

- Spark
- Storm
- HAMA
- Giraph

The integration of Spark with YARN

Spark is a distributed computing framework that uses in-memory primitives to process data available in a data store. It provides an in-memory representation of data to be processed and it is well suited for various machine learning algorithms. Spark allows easy connection to different data stores such as HDFS, Cassandra, and Amazon S3.

There are several companies that use Spark for big data processing. The complete list of companies and their use cases is available at `https://cwiki.apache.org/confluence/display/SPARK/Powered+By+Spark`.

Spark has two components: `SparkContext` (`Driver`) and `Executor`. `SparkContext` is a master service that connects with a cluster manager and acquires resources for `Executor` services on worker nodes. For cluster management, Spark supports YARN, Apache Mesos and an in-built standalone cluster manager.

In this section, we'll discuss how Spark is integrated with YARN and how you can submit Spark-YARN applications on a Hadoop-YARN cluster. This book does not focus on Spark components and its architecture. To read more about the technology, you can refer to the official website at `https://spark.apache.org/`.

Running Spark on YARN

YARN allows execution of user-defined applications over a cluster. Spark defines its own application master to interact with ResourceManager and manage the execution of Spark application tasks over the cluster. A client submits a Spark application to the YARN ResourceManager service. The ResourceManager accepts the application request and starts an ApplicationMaster service for the new application. The ApplicationMaster runs as a first YARN container and manages the application execution. The ResourceManager is responsible for scheduling applications submitted to the cluster. It allocates YARN containers for `Executor` services.

The following diagram represents a Spark-YARN cluster:

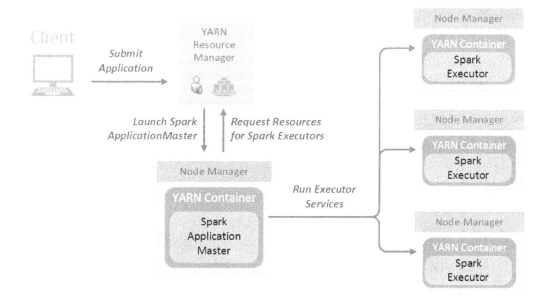

As discussed earlier, Spark runs a `Driver` service `SparkContext` as a master service. The node on which the driver service runs depends on the deployment mode specified during startup. There are two deploy modes for running Spark-on-YARN:

- `yarn-client`: In this mode, the `Driver` service runs within the client process that initiates the application. The ApplicationMaster process is responsible for acquiring resources from ResourceManager only. The `yarn-client` mode is useful for interactive Spark applications that require user input, such as Spark-shell.

- `yarn-cluster`: In this mode, the `Driver` service runs within the Spark ApplicationMaster process, that is, with a YARN container. The ApplicationMaster is responsible for both, requesting resources from the ResourceManager and driving the application execution. The client may not maintain the session for the application's entire lifetime. This mode is widely used for long production jobs that do not require user input.

You can download the Spark-Hadoop bundle from the official website of Spark at `http://spark.apache.org/downloads.html`.

You need to choose the package type based on your Hadoop version.

Spark requires Hadoop client configuration files to read the address of YARN ResourceManager and other Hadoop-YARN configurations. To submit Spark applications on YARN, you can use the `spark-submit` command available at `$SPARK_HOME/bin` as shown in the following lines of command:

```
export HADOOP_CONF_DIR=XXX
$SPARK_HOME/bin/spark-submit --class
org.apache.spark.examples.SparkPi --master <deploy-mode> --num-
executors 3 --driver-memory 512m --executor-memory 512m --executor-
cores 1 $SPARK_HOME/lib/spark-examples*.jar 10
```

You need to replace `<deploy-mode>` with either `yarn-cluster` or `yarn-client`. The preceding command will instantiate the `org.apache.spark.deploy.SparkSubmit` class and launch the Spark `Driver` service based on the node based on the deploy mode. You can configure the number of executors and memory for each executor using the `submit` command options.

The output snippets of the preceding command are described as follows:

- **Initializing ApplicationSubmissionContext**:

    ```
    15/03/10 02:15:43 INFO Client: Requesting a new application
    from cluster with 1 NodeManagers

    15/03/10 02:15:43 INFO Client: Verifying our application has
    not requested more than the maximum memory capability of the
    cluster (8192 MB per container)

    15/03/10 02:15:43 INFO Client: Will allocate AM container,
    with 896 MB memory including 384 MB overhead

    15/03/10 02:15:43 INFO Client: Setting up container launch
    context for our AM

    15/03/10 02:15:43 INFO Client: Preparing resources for our AM
    container

    15/03/10 02:15:43 INFO Client: Source and destination file
    systems are the same. Not copying file:/opt/spark/spark-1.2.1-
    bin-hadoop2.4/lib/spark-assembly-1.2.1-hadoop2.4.0.jar

    15/03/10 02:15:43 INFO Client: Source and destination file
    systems are the same. Not copying file:/opt/spark/spark-1.2.1-
    bin-hadoop2.4/lib/spark-examples-1.2.1-hadoop2.4.0.jar

    15/03/10 02:15:43 INFO Client: Setting up the launch
    environment for our AM container

    15/03/10 02:15:43 INFO SecurityManager: Changing view acls to:
    root
    ```

```
15/03/10 02:15:43 INFO SecurityManager: Changing modify acls
to: root
15/03/10 02:15:43 INFO SecurityManager: SecurityManager:
authentication disabled; uiacls disabled; users with view
permissions: Set(root); users with modify permissions:
Set(root)
```

- **Submitting application to ResourceManager:**

```
15/03/10 02:15:44 INFO Client: Submitting application 3 to
ResourceManager
15/03/10 02:15:44 INFO YarnClientImpl: Submitted application
application_1425928419662_0003
15/03/10 02:15:45 INFO Client: Application report for
application_1425928419662_0003 (state: ACCEPTED)
```

- **Launching ApplicationMaster service:**

```
15/03/10 02:16:19 INFO Client:
        client token: N/A
        diagnostics: N/A
ApplicationMaster host: 192.168.56.102
ApplicationMaster RPC port: 0
        queue: default
        start time: 1425933944023
        final status: UNDEFINED
        tracking URL: http://localhost:8088/proxy/
application_1425928419662_0003/
        user: root
```

You can also view the application status on the YARN's ResourceManager UI at `http://<ResourceManagerHost>:8088/`:

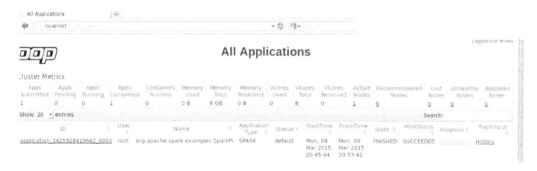

To read more about Spark on YARN and other configuration parameters, you can refer to the following links:

`http://spark.apache.org/docs/1.3.0/running-on-yarn.html`

`http://blog.cloudera.com/blog/2014/05/apache-spark-resource-management-and-yarn-app-models/`

`https://spark.apache.org/docs/1.3.0/submitting-applications.html`

The integration of Storm with YARN

Storm is a distributed computational and processing framework, which was developed to process streaming data in real time. It has been released as open source. It is useful for continuous monitoring of processes and running machine learning algorithms. Storm can process millions of records per second on a single node and is widely used for low-latency processing.

Storm has two main services: `Nimbus` (master) and `Supervisor` (slave). Storm requires Zookeeper component for co-ordination between the `Nimbus` and `Supervisor` services. The Storm bundle contains a `storm.yaml` configuration file. The file contains information related to the `Nimbus` server and the Zookeeper quorum. Similar to Spark, this book does not focus on the architecture and the components of Storm. To read more about Storm, you can refer to the official website at `https://storm.apache.org/`.

Companies such as GroupOn, The Weather Channel, Twitter, Yahoo, and so on are using Storm. To get the full list and their use cases, you can refer to the official documentation at `https://storm.apache.org/documentation/Powered-By.html`.

Similar to Hadoop MapReduce application, Storm executes topologies over a cluster of nodes. As a distributed framework, Storm needs to manage the cluster resources and schedule the execution of topologies efficiently. The Storm services (`Nimbus` / `Supervisor` / `Core`) run as YARN containers and are managed by the ApplicationMaster for Storm (`MasterServer` service).

The following diagram shows the bird's eye view of Storm's architecture over YARN:

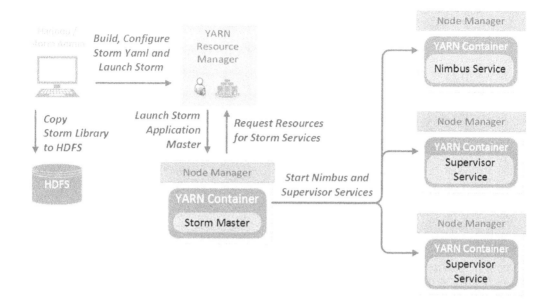

Running Storm on YARN

Before running Storm over a YARN cluster, you need to make sure that Storm dependencies are already installed on all the cluster nodes. If you wish to read more about Storm cluster mode deployment, you can refer to the official documentation at `https://storm.apache.org/documentation/Setting-up-a-Storm-cluster.html`.

The following are the dependencies for the current stable Storm release (0.9.3):

- Java 7
- Python 2.6.6 or later

Running a Storm-Yarn cluster is a simple five-step process, as shown in the following diagram:

Create a Zookeeper quorum

Apache Zookeeper is a coordination service for distributed applications such as Storm, Kafka, HBase, and so on. A running Zookeeper quorum is required by Nimbus service to manage the available supervisor nodes in the cluster. You need to deploy a Zookeeper quorum (either standalone or clustered mode). To deploy a standalone Zookeeper quorum, you can refer to any of these blogs at `http://www.protechskills.com/big-data/hadoop-ecosystem/zookeeper/zookeeper-standalone-installation` or `http://zookeeper.apache.org/doc/trunk/zookeeperStarted.html`.

Download, extract, and prepare the Storm bundle

You can download a Storm bundle from the official download page at `https://storm.apache.org/downloads.html` or from the Apache archive. Extract the download Storm bundle on your node using the `tar` command.

```
wgethttp://archive.apache.org/dist/storm/apache-storm-0.9.3/apache-storm-
0.9.3.tar.gz
tar -xvzf apache-storm-0.9.3.tar.gz
```

Storm-Yarn is an open source project available on GitHub. You can access the project at `https://github.com/yahoo/storm-yarn`. You can download the source code as a ZIP file from the GitHub page we mentioned. You will need to extract the file contents and change the current working directory to the extracted folder.

```
wget https://github.com/yahoo/storm-yarn/archive/master.zip
unzip storm-yarn-master.zip
cd storm-yarn-master
```

To prepare the bundle for YARN, you need to execute a script and create a ZIP file (`storm.zip`) containing Storm libraries. You need to execute the following commands to prepare a `storm` ZIP file:

```
/create-tarball.sh lib/storm.zip
cd lib
unzip storm.zip
cp storm-0.9.0-wip21 storm-0.9.3
zip -r storm.zip storm-0.9.3
```

Copy Storm ZIP to HDFS

You need to create a directory for the Storm library in Hadoop HDFS. Log in to a Hadoop node or a Hadoop client node and execute the following commands to create the required directory and copy the `storm.zip` file to HDFS:

```
hdfsdfs -mkdir -p '/lib/storm/0.9.3'
hadoop fs -put '/opt/storm-yarn-
master/lib/storm.zip''/lib/storm/0.9.3/'
```

Configuring the storm.yaml file

Before running the `launch` command, you need to configure the `storm.yaml` file. You can edit the file in the configuration folder `apache-storm-0.9.3/conf` of the `storm` folder extracted in the step 2 (a).

You need to add the configuration for your Zookeeper quorum, the initial number of `supervisor` nodes required and the size of the Storm master service (the ApplicationMaster for Strom) in MB using the following properties:

```
storm.zookeeper.servers:
  - "server1"
master.initial-num-supervisors: 1
master.container.size-mb: 256
```

Launching the Storm-YARN cluster

To launch the Storm-Yarn cluster, you will need to execute the following `storm-yarn` executable in the `bin` folder of the bundle extracted in step 2 (b).

```
bin/storm-yarn launch apache-storm-0.9.3/conf/storm.yaml
```

You can refer to the ResourceManager UI of Hadoop-YARN cluster `http://<Resou rceManagerHost>:8088/` to view details of a new application related to the Storm-Yarn cluster:

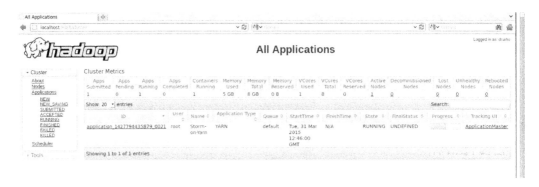

You can also execute the `jps` command on the nodes to view the `MasterServer`, `Nimbus`, `core` and `Supervisor` services running in the cluster:

Managing Storm on YARN

The `storm-yarn` executable file that was used in step 5 in the preceding section to launch the Storm-Yarn cluster is used to manage the cluster as well.

Here are a few options for the `storm-yarn` command:

- `help`
- `launch`
- `shutdown`
- `addSupervisors-setStormConfig`
- `getStormConfig`
- `startNimbus`
- `stopNimbus-startUI`
- `stopUI`
- `startSupervisors`
- `stopSupervisors`

The command to get the `storm.yaml` configuration file on the local filesystem is:

`storm-yarn getStormConfig –appId <Application-ID> --output <path to storm.yaml>`

You need to replace `<Application-ID>` with the actual application ID retrieved from the ResourceManager UI. You also need to specify the local filesystem path to store the `storm.yaml` file. The final command will look like this:

`storm-yarn getStormConfig --appId application_23232344_001 --output /home/hduser/storm.yaml`

> To read more about these commands and arguments required, you can refer to the StormMasterCommand class at `https://github.com/yahoo/storm-yarn/blob/master/src/main/java/com/yahoo/storm/yarn/StormMasterCommand.java`.
>
> Similar to the MapReduce in Hadoop, Storm master communicates with the ResourceManager using `StormAMRMClient` service. To read about the service, you can refer to the class at `https://github.com/yahoo/storm-yarn/blob/master/src/main/java/com/yahoo/storm/yarn/StormAMRMClient.java`.

The integration of HAMA and Giraph with YARN

Apache HAMA is a distributed computing framework based on Bulk Synchronous Parallel algorithms. It provides high performance computing for performance-intensive, scientific, and iterative algorithms such as Matrix, Graph, and Machine Learning.

HAMA consists of three major components:

* BSPMaster
* GroomServers
* Zookeeper

Deploying HAMA with YARN is a simple process and you can refer to the following references:

* http://wiki.apache.org/hama/GettingStartedYARN
* http://wiki.apache.org/hama/GettingStarted/Properties

Apache Giraph is a framework for iterative processing of semi-structured graphs. It is inspired from Google's Pregel, which is also a graph processing framework. Giraph is also based on a Bulk Synchronous Parallel model of distributed computing.

For more details on Giraph, you can refer to the official website at http://giraph.apache.org/.

Initially, Giraph was used with the MapReduce framework for Hadoop 1.x. There were a few concerns, such as:

* Defining cluster resource requirements as Map / Reduce slots
* No control over resource allocation
* Inappropriate UI to monitor the progress and statistics

Use of YARN allows Giraph to define its own ApplicationMaster and resource allocations policies. Giraph applications can be easily monitored using a customized web application for GiraphApplicationMaster as well.

To read more about submitting Giraph jobs to the Hadoop-YARN cluster, you can refer to the documentation at http://giraph.apache.org/quick_start.html.

Summary

YARN is used as a generic resource manager for distributed applications. YARN allows easy resource scheduling and application execution over a cluster of nodes. YARN is being integrated with different big data technologies such as Apache Storm, Spark, and so on. In this chapter, you learned about the Spark-YARN architecture and how you can submit Spark jobs on YARN. You also learned about the integration of Storm on YARN and how you can manage the storm services through YARN. This chapter also covered a brief overview of the integration of HAMA and Giraph with YARN.

Index

A

S

Thank you for buying
Learning YARN

About Packt Publishing

Packt, pronounced 'packed', published its first book, *Mastering phpMyAdmin for Effective MySQL Management*, in April 2004, and subsequently continued to specialize in publishing highly focused books on specific technologies and solutions.

Our books and publications share the experiences of your fellow IT professionals in adapting and customizing today's systems, applications, and frameworks. Our solution-based books give you the knowledge and power to customize the software and technologies you're using to get the job done. Packt books are more specific and less general than the IT books you have seen in the past. Our unique business model allows us to bring you more focused information, giving you more of what you need to know, and less of what you don't.

Packt is a modern yet unique publishing company that focuses on producing quality, cutting-edge books for communities of developers, administrators, and newbies alike. For more information, please visit our website at www.packtpub.com.

About Packt Open Source

In 2010, Packt launched two new brands, Packt Open Source and Packt Enterprise, in order to continue its focus on specialization. This book is part of the Packt Open Source brand, home to books published on software built around open source licenses, and offering information to anybody from advanced developers to budding web designers. The Open Source brand also runs Packt's Open Source Royalty Scheme, by which Packt gives a royalty to each open source project about whose software a book is sold.

Writing for Packt

We welcome all inquiries from people who are interested in authoring. Book proposals should be sent to author@packtpub.com. If your book idea is still at an early stage and you would like to discuss it first before writing a formal book proposal, then please contact us; one of our commissioning editors will get in touch with you.

We're not just looking for published authors; if you have strong technical skills but no writing experience, our experienced editors can help you develop a writing career, or simply get some additional reward for your expertise.

YARN Essentials

ISBN: 978-1-78439-173-7   Paperback: 176 pages

A comprehensive, hands-on guide to install, administer, and configure settings in YARN

1. Learn the inner workings of YARN and how its robust and generic framework enables optimal resource utilization across multiple applications.

2. Get to grips with single and multi-node installation, administration, and real-time distributed application development.

3. A step-by-step self-learning guide to help you perform optimal resource utilization in a cluster.

Hadoop Backup and Recovery Solutions

ISBN: 978-1-78328-904-2   Paperback: 206 pages

Learn the best strategies for data recovery from Hadoop backup clusters and troubleshoot problems

1. Learn the fundamentals of Hadoop's backup needs, recovery strategy, and troubleshooting.

2. Determine common failure points, intimate HBase, and explore different backup techniques to resolve failures.

3. Explore common issues and their solutions using in-depth knowledge of Hadoop.

Please check **www.PacktPub.com** for information on our titles

Mastering Hadoop

ISBN: 978-1-78398-364-3   Paperback: 374 pages

Go beyond the basics and master the next generation of Hadoop data processing platforms

1. Learn how to optimize Hadoop MapReduce, Pig and Hive.

2. Dive into YARN and learn how it can integrate Storm with Hadoop.

3. Understand how Hadoop can be deployed on the cloud and gain insights into analytics with Hadoop.

Hadoop MapReduce v2 Cookbook
Second Edition

ISBN: 978-1-78328-547-1   Paperback: 322 pages

Explore the Hadoop MapReduce v2 ecosystem to gain insights from very large datasets

1. Process large and complex datasets using next generation Hadoop.

2. Install, configure, and administer MapReduce programs and learn what's new in MapReduce v2.

3. More than 90 Hadoop MapReduce recipes presented in a simple and straightforward manner, with step-by-step instructions and real-world examples.

Please check **www.PacktPub.com** for information on our titles

www.ingramcontent.com/pod-product-compliance
Lightning Source LLC
Chambersburg PA
CBHW060528060326

40690CB00017B/3420